A HANDBOOK OF FLY-TYING

Plate I   Frontispiece

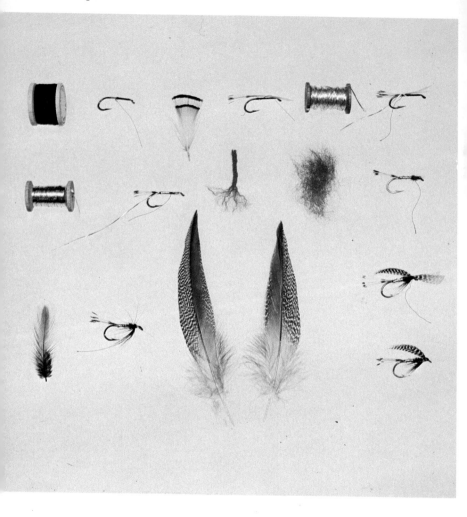

DRESSING A "PETER ROSS"

Start by running-on a smooth bed of black tying silk. Then tie in a few fibres of Golden Pheasant "tippet" for the tail, and secure the oval silver tinsel for ribbing.

Form the rear half of the body with flat silver tinsel and use dubbed scarlet Seal's fur for the front half. Rib the whole body with the oval tinsel.

Tie in a black hen hackle , and finally tie a wing formed from segments of Teal shoulder.

A HANDBOOK
OF FLY-TYING

by

DENIS H. ARDLEY

SECOND EDITION

H. F. & G. WITHERBY LTD

Second Edition first published 1985
This paperback edition first published 1989 by
H. F. & G. WITHERBY LTD
14 Henrietta Street, London WC2E 8QJ

© Denis H. Ardley 1985

A CIP catalogue record for this book is
available from the British Library.

ISBN 0 85493 177 5

Printed in Great Britain

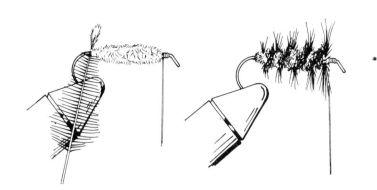

Contents

PART ONE
TOOLS AND MATERIALS

PART TWO
FLY-DRESSING PROCESSES
AND TECHNIQUES

PART THREE
PRACTICAL WORK

PART FOUR
FEATHERS AND FUR

PART FIVE
BOOKS AND ORGANISATIONS

Colour Plates

INTRODUCTION

From several years of experience in teaching beginners from scratch I feel that too many books on the subject of fly-tying have two disadvantageous tendencies. The first is that their authors tend to assume that their readers already have a working knowledge of the subject. This is not necessarily true; indeed in the majority of cases the beginner is completely befogged by much of the terminology. The second is that they concentrate on the tying of specific patterns of fly rather than on the generality of the actual processes and techniques involved in building up a fly.

As far as possible "hearsay evidence" has been avoided. All the various processes described in the pages that follow have been thoroughly tried out and none of them should be beyond the practical capabilities of the normally competent and painstaking person.

I have attempted to produce first a guide in easily understood language from which a novice can if necessary learn the basic processes of fly-dressing if he has not been fortunate enough to find some more experienced person to teach him by way of personal demonstration.

Secondly, not only for the learner who may be in the process of receiving individual or class instruction but also for the more experienced hand, a convenient record or notebook expanding what he may have learned from his instructor or from the experience of others.

Finally, to stress the enjoyment and satisfaction to be derived from "do-it-yourself" fly-dressing.

The art of producing a lure which either imitates some natural living creature or which is merely an object that attracts the fish or provokes them to attack it goes back into unrecorded history. The person who develops an interest in this historical aspect will doubtless seek to widen his knowledge, to which end a study of the works of the past masters of the craft will prove rewarding.

"WHY TIE YOUR OWN FLIES?"
The fisherman, however accomplished he may be in the skills of cautious approach, his "reading" or assessment of the water and his accuracy of casting will find his enjoyment of the sport enhanced beyond measure if his fish has been caught on a fly of his own making and even more so if it is of a pattern of his own devising.

The man who ties his own can please himself as to style and scale of dressing and render himself independent of the usually overdressed "shop" article.

A point to bear in mind is that of cost. Fly-tying as a trade has a high labour content and few of its processes lend themselves readily to mechanisation. In other words a high percentage of the cost of a "bought" fly represents wages and as these continue to rise the price of the commercial article is bound to increase disproportionately.

The other major advantage might be described as therapeutic: fly-tying is a pleasant and absorbing hobby. Strangely enough, although it calls for considerable concentration and precision of work it also affords an enormous degree of mental relaxation; the irritations of the day fade into their proper degree of unimportance when you sit down at your fly-tying bench and concentrate on your current masterpiece, the only extraneous thoughts being those of anticipation of good fishing days to come and of the opportunity of trying out the fly itself.

It has, too, what might be termed a "social" benefit; anglers in general and fly-dressers in particular are a very friendly race and where two or three are gathered together there before very long will be animated but amicable discussion and argument and the exchange of ideas and experiences.

STARTING TO LEARN
The potential recruit to fly-dressing may feel some hesitation about embarking on such a handicraft, particularly if he or she is past the first flush of youth, but let this be no deterrent. While admittedly the younger person will possibly find it easier, many people who have not taken it up until their fifties or sixties reach a high

standard of proficiency in a comparatively short time. Although some, such as instrument-makers or other skilled engineers and not forgetting good needlewomen, start off of course with a big advantage, few of the processes in fly-tying are beyond the scope of the learner, provided he has the full muscular control of the fingers and reasonable eyesight (if necessary with the aid of spectacles).

The beginner would be well advised nevertheless to seek the assistance of those more experienced, either by way of having personal tuition from a friend or by joining an instructional class organised by his Local Education Authority or similar body, but standards of teaching do vary.

The various processes and techniques of fly-dressing have been set out in the pages that follow in what I consider to be a logical sequence and when these have been practised and mastered the dresser should be able to reproduce any fly or lure which he may see or about which he may read in the future.

At the end of this book he will find a list of other books from which he can obtain the "recipes" for specific dressings and which will assist him in his study and practice.

I have deliberately refrained from quoting prices of tools or materials used in fly-tying in view of their rapid variation (usually upwards). The reader can get current figures from the catalogues of the firms supplying these articles.

The opportunity has been taken in this second edition to make various revisions and corrections to bring the book up-to-date.

Hatfield Peverel
March, 1985

DENIS H. ARDLEY

ACKNOWLEDGEMENTS

This book was written in intervals between fishing and would never have reached anything like completion without the help of many other people, to whom I owe a deep debt of gratitude.

Beginning at the beginning, my interest in fly-fishing was triggered off in a prisoner-of-war camp in Italy in 1942 where I had the good fortune to meet Tony Ogden-Smith, whose family firm made fine rods and tackle.

I have derived immense enjoyment from fly-fishing and most of this has been due to Edward Arnold in so generously allowing me to fish his beat of the river Usk. To fish in such delightful surroundings is indeed a privilege.

On the fly-tying side my thanks are due first to Geoffrey Bucknall, from whom I not only acquired a certain degree of competence but the ability to learn more. Not only a fine craftsman, he is a first-class instructor blessed with the twin gifts of infinite patience and the capability of expressing himself clearly in both written and spoken English.

Next comes John Veniard, late Managing Director of Veniards' suppliers of fly-tyers' materials. No fly-tyer goes to John for help or advice without receiving it in full measure, given in his inimitable cheerful and kindly way.

Five good friends of mine, Simon Bayley, Trevor McCann, John Poole, Peter Thomasson and Bernard Wakeham, not only good fly-dressers but experienced practical fish-catching anglers, all gave up time to wade through the original draft of the book and made constructive suggestions for its improvement.

I owe considerable gratitude too to the members of my evening-classes in fly-tying at Chelmsford who so amply proved the truth of the theory that the best way of learning any subject is to teach it. In many ways this book is their work, as it was their questions that prompted me to write it.

On the actual production side my thanks are due to Antony Witherby for his advice and guidance to a novice writer, to John

Tarlton for the photographs and to Herbert Marshall for the clear drawings in the text.

Lastly, but by no means least, I must acknowledge the constant help and encouragement given by my wife.

PART I

TOOLS AND MATERIALS

1

TOOLS AND EQUIPMENT

When a beginner sets out to learn any trade or handicraft the first things which are shown and explained to him are the tools which he will be handling and the characteristics of the various materials with which he will be working. So it is with fly-dressing, so let us commence with a study of these.

BENCH
Just as the carpenter needs a bench of suitable height and the clerk a comfortable desk, so the first essential is a firm working-surface with adequate room to set out the tools and materials to be used on each particular occasion.

While the working height is important, there are certain other things that can cause the fly-dresser to use immoderate language; the first of these is the tool that rolls off the bench and under a heavy piece of furniture just when it is wanted! (The most frequent offenders here are the dubbing-needle and the cap of the varnish-bottle). Be careful therefore to check that your working-surface is firm and level.

Fly-dressing is "fine" work, so the siting of the table or bench and the quality and direction of the light available are important in order to avoid unnecessary eye-strain.

It is well worth while to place a sheet of white paper or smooth plastic about one foot square on the bench where the vice is attached; this not only affords a good "sight-screen" but at the end of each session you can pick up the sheet by the corners and tip all the waste bits of feathers, etc. into the wastepaper basket. (Textile material is not recommended for this purpose as the bits tend to stick to a "nap" surface).

Some tyers even go to the length of laying a white dust-sheet under their bench and chair. This means that anything dropped accidentally, especially a hook, can readily be seen.

VICE

While some very experienced fly-dressers can tie flies with the hook merely held in the fingers, the basic need for most of us is a properly designed fly-tyer's vice which can be securely clamped to the table or bench, leaving both hands free for handling the tools and manipulating the materials.

This will be by far the most expensive item of your equipment and, as with most things, the better the quality you can afford the longer it will last and the more efficiently will it perform. If therefore the beginner is serious in his determination to become a proficient fly-dresser he would be well advised to purchase a good model.

A wide range of choice is offered.

First, there is the pattern which is virtually a scaled-down version of the ordinary workshop vice. This can prove difficult for a beginner to use; its great disadvantage is, as the jaws are vertical, there is very little scope for manipulation of the fingers when the hook is clamped in position.

Obviously therefore it is more practical if the "head" carrying the jaws is angled over like a gallows so as to provide this working space for the fingers. It is of additional advantage if this working head is adjustable for height and direction.

The chuck or jaws holding the hook can be tightened either by means of a milled screw or by a quick-release cam lever. The latter type is preferable as the screw tends to jam with wear and can prove difficult to release.

It will be of further benefit if the head of the vice can be rotated about its own axis; for example, when one "leg" of a double hook is placed in the jaws the head can be rotated (and secured) so that the whole upper surface of the hook is in the horizontal plane.

Whichever type is purchased it is most important to check that the jaws are made of well-hardened steel, that the slot for the hook is cut straight and that the jaws fit flush and provide a firm grip of the hook. Ill-fitting jaws that allow the hook to slip, usually at a crucial moment in the proceedings, can be a great source of irritation and lead to spoiled work.

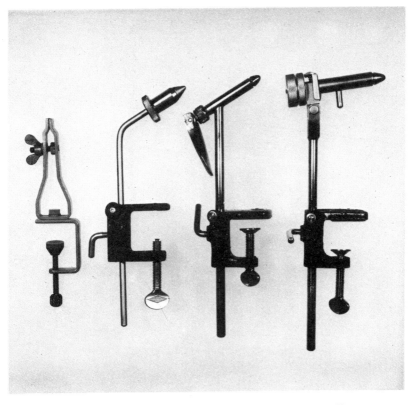

SOME FLY-DRESSERS' VICES (VENIARDS')

It is a commonsense practice to glue a piece of felt or baize over the jaws of the clamp which fixes the vice to the bench. This will avoid the possibility of scratching or marking a polished surface if the vice is used on a table or other furniture.

Our fly-dresser may well be a do-it-yourself handyman in which case he can avoid this major outlay on a vice. While a perfectly serviceable article can be made from a small "pin" vice, a length of steel rod about ¼-inch in diameter and a crude table clamp, the more skilled toolmaker can produce an instrument incorporating all the desirable features.

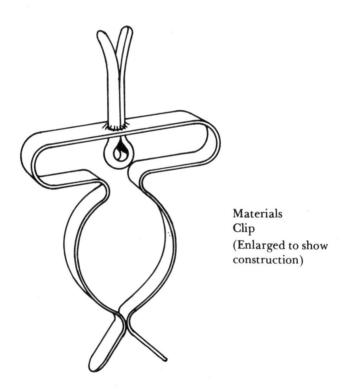

Materials
Clip
(Enlarged to show
construction)

A useful addition to any vice is a clip which can be slipped on to the head or barrel of the vice to hold the dressing materials out of the way until they are required. This can be bought or a simple clip can be made by any amateur. Get a spring "Terry" clip that will grip the barrel comfortably and insert through the screw hole a split-pin cut to about ½-inch long. Open up the ends of the pin slightly and secure the pin in the hole with a blob of solder; sealing-wax or an adhesive such as "Araldite" will serve equally well.

There are also on the market small "pocket" vices which can be held in the hand, presumably for the benefit of the man who wants to tie his flies at the waterside when he thinks he knows what the fish are taking. While I have the utmost respect and admiration for such expertise there are to my mind at least four disadvantages attaching to this practice:

First, it is a waste of good fishing time.

Secondly, in order to secure the "match" required the angler would have to carry half his fly-tying stores with him.

Thirdly, he will make a much more satisfactory job of it if he works on a firm surface without the risk of wind dispersing his materials.

And lastly, the fish will probably have changed their minds as to diet by the time he has finished!

The sensible answer is to stock up the fly-box with plenty of one's favourite flies in a variety of sizes.

HACKLE-PLIERS

These are clips of spring steel with flat jaws which assist in holding and handling various types of material. It is advisable to have two pairs, medium (2 inches long) and small (1½ inches).

Check that the jaws bed down flush and that their edges are not sharp or they will cut delicate material; smooth down any such sharp edges with a fine file. It will also help if one arm of the jaws is covered with a ¼-inch length of cycle valve rubber. Renew this as soon as it shows signs of perishing or becoming sticky.

SCISSORS

Two pairs are needed. For cutting or trimming the finer materials the best are the type with long handles and short points which can be straight or curved according to taste. These are known in the cutlery trade as "cuticle" scissors.

For cutting tinsel and stouter materials a somewhat less delicate pair are used. Those illustrated are known in the trade as "embroidery" scissors.

Good quality scissors are very expensive but they are well worth their cost; there is no more false economy than the purchase of cheap (usually foreign-made) scissors. Always see that your scissors cut right up to their points.

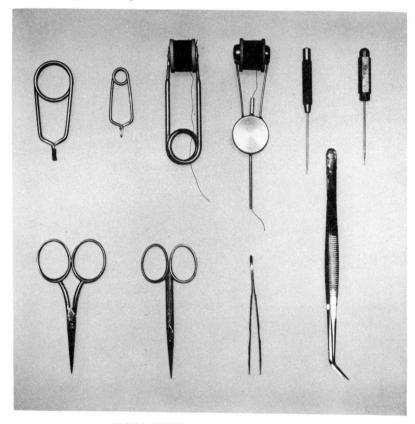

TOOLS USED IN FLY-DRESSING

Top: Hackle-Pliers   Bobbin-Holder   Dubbing-Needles
       Medium and   Veniards and Tubular   The right-hand one
       Small   home-made with
                                        hexagonal handle to
                                        prevent rolling

Lower: Scissors, Embroidery and Cuticle   Tweezers   Dental Packing
                                                              Forceps

DUBBING-NEEDLE

This implement has many uses, for dividing feathers, picking out fibres that may have been caught up in the tying and for applying minute drops of varnish to the heads of completed flies.

All it consists of is a stout needle set in a handle. While they can be bought, one can easily be made by jamming the butt of a darning-needle into a handle of cork, wood, plastic or metal.

The built-in disadvantage of a handle of circular section will immediately become apparent if the bench is not level and the tool rolls off. A handle of square or hexagonal section will obviate this, as will the grinding of a "flat" on one side of a cylindrical handle.

TWEEZERS

These will be needed for picking up and handling some of the smaller items of material. While my own preference is for a pair with pointed ends, those with square or "spade" ends are doubtless equally effective.

A serviceable pair can be bought quite cheaply but if you are prepared to spend somewhat more the ideal is a pair of dental "packing" forceps with fine points bent over at an angle, these are catalogued as "College Tweezers".

BOBBIN-HOLDERS

These are such useful tools that I have no hesitation in including them in the "basic" list. The bobbin-holder has three particular points in its favour; not only does it avoid the necessity of clipping on hackle-pliers at various stages of the dressing, but it keeps the tying-silk, especially the paler shades, cleaner than when the reel is held in a moist hand. It also saves cutting off several inches of waste silk every time a fly is finished off.

The cheaper model resembles the hackle-pliers: it is made of spring steel and the jaws carry small lugs which hold the standard size reel of tying-silk under the correct tension. The silk passes from the reel through two holes drilled in the loop of the holder.

In the other type the silk is fed through a short length of fine-gauge metal tubing. This makes it easier for the dresser to manipulate the silk under the exposed hook-points, particularly when dealing with double or treble hooks. In some makes the metal tube is lined with nylon or plastic but I have found that after a time the tying-silk tends to wear a groove in the lining.

The only criticisms of either of these instruments are first that the grip afforded by the lugs is sometimes not sufficiently firm to maintain proper tension on the silk and secondly it may occasionally be found when using a new bobbin-holder for the first time that the edges of the holes or tube through which the silk passes are rough and will fray the silk. The first of these faults can be remedied by twisting a rubber band over the arms of the holder and the second by reaming the apertures smooth with a "needle" file.

OTHER TOOLS

The suppliers' catalogues abound in items which can aid the fly-dresser in his work, including an ingenious tool for effecting a neat "whip-finish" which may help the novice who has difficulty in doing this with his fingers (see page 54). There are also cutters using standard pattern razor-blades for trimming to size hackles which are too wide and gauges for measuring exactly matching segments of wing feather. I would stress that they are not really necessary.

Under this heading of tools and equipment we can include partitioned transparent plastic boxes. Use a large one with movable partitions to hold in logical order all the materials required for a particular job. Another smaller box with fixed divisions will hold in its various compartments any odds and ends of feathers, floss-silk and tinsels which may come in handy on a later occasion. Such a "snippets" box can prove very useful.

For those who find that their eyesight calls for it, a magnifier of some sort can be of assistance at various stages of the work. While the most satisfactory type is that with a heavy base and a flexible stem which enables the user to position the lens where he wants it, some people prefer a more portable form of magnifier in the form of spectacles or even a watchmaker's eyeglass, which can be obtained quite cheaply.

The final item which every fly-dresser's kit should include is a clean piece of absorbent cloth. This has many uses, the chief of these being to wipe sticky wax from the fingers and to clean surplus varnish from the dubbing-needle; one's jacket or trousers are not the proper tools for this!

The beginner, when he starts to collect his kit of tools, should get his teacher or an experienced tyer to accompany him when he goes to the tackle-shop. Some of the equipment now being marketed, even including some more expensive items, is leaving the factory without the degree of quality control required.

2

HOOKS

Today's fly-dresser works in an ever-widening range of materials and his task will be rendered easier if he is fully conversant with their differing characteristics.

We will now deal with these in some detail and as the hook is the frame or skeleton of all our work it merits pride of place in consideration as a "material".

Once again the accent is on quality. If you have taken the time and trouble to learn the art and to tie flies neatly and well it is a pity to waste those hardly acquired talents on inferior material.

This question of quality is a perennial subject for grumbling amongst anglers. What must be borne in mind is that the better manufacturers with higher standards of quality control are able to export the bulk of their production, the really good Redditch-made hook having a high reputation abroad. This, while cold comfort to the fly-dresser or angler who may find difficulty in obtaining exactly what he wants, is doubtless in the national interest.

Hooks made by such a good manufacturer will avoid the faults which one is apt to encounter all too often, the main examples of which are:

1. Badly tempered metal. Either the hook is soft, in which case it will straighten out under strain (usually in the fish of a lifetime), or it is brittle which may mean the equally infuriating experience of the wire actually snapping.

2. Badly formed eyes. The cut end of the wire has not been brought right flush with the shank, so that there is a space (often bounded on one side by a sharp edge) into which the tying-silk can slip with the consequent likelihood of fraying and breaking.

It is of no use trying to close this gap with pliers or a hammer; it is more satisfactory to clip off the offending eye and to use the hook as a "blind" (q.v.). Incidentally, don't do this with wire-cutters; the eye will fly off like a bullet. Just press the eye with a pair of pliers and it will break off cleanly.

23

3. Barbs. These are frequently too "rank", i.e. they are cut too deep. This is not only a source of weakness but also tends to prevent quick and efficient penetration. A hook of this sort will break at the barb at the slightest strain; indeed it may break in the vice just as you have finished what would otherwise have been a perfect example of the fly-dresser's art. (Don't throw this away in disgust: it will always make a nice hat-ornament!)

The answer to all these problems is to find a good brand of hook and to stick to that brand as far as possible.

This is a logical stage at which to include a reminder of the terms given to the various parts of the hook:

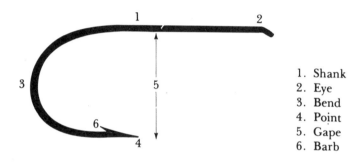

1. Shank
2. Eye
3. Bend
4. Point
5. Gape
6. Barb

EYES

These are usually formed by bending the wire in a circular loop so that the cut end lies snug and close against the shank: this is commonly known as a "ball" eye.

In the case of the more expensive "tapered" eye the cut end is tapered down and the whole (pear-shaped) eye is a closer and neater job.

In the traditional pattern of salmon-hook the end of the wire is flattened and brought round as a tapered tang or bar parallel with the shank. This is sometimes referred to as a "looped" eye.

The loop of wire forming the eye can be bent upwards at an angle of about 30° from the shank, in which case it is listed as "turned-up-eye", "t.u.e." or "up-eyed".

Conversely, the hook with the eye-loop bent downwards at a similar angle is referred to as "turned-down-eye", "t.d.e." or "down-eyed".

When this eye-loop has not been bent up or down but has been left in the same horizontal plane as the shank it is known as a "flat" or "straight" eye.

As a general practice, the turned-up eye is used for dry flies while the wet fly is usually dressed on a down-eyed hook, the underlying theory being that the bent-up eye helps to lift the fly while the down-eye acts in a similar manner to the diving-vane on a plug bait.

However, to add to the confusion with which this particular subject is so liberally endowed, salmon-flies (which are usually fished well and truly "wet") are traditionally dressed on a hook with an upturned eye!

The point of dressing flies on up- or down-eyed hooks becomes apparent if a "Turle' or "Cairnton" knot is used to secure the fly to the end of the leader. In such cases the actual knot is tied round the neck of the shank and only the single strand of the leader passes through the eye: thus the leader always stays in line with the shank of the hook. For the angler whose prowess in tying knots does not extend beyond threading the leader through the eye and securing it with a tucked half-blood knot this question of whether eyes should turn up or down is probably largely academic.

When making up lures with multiple hooks, it is only the foremost hook which need carry an eye for attachment to the leader; the remainder are better with a plain shank with no eye. These latter are commonly known as "blind" hooks.

SHANKS

These come in various proportional lengths and thicknesses. For example, the ordinary trout-fly calls for a hook fairly short and light in the wire, and a heavier grade is needed for sunk flies and lures. For Mayflies a hook with a long shank, although still light in the wire, is used.

A fly of the "streamer" type has a stouter long-shanked hook and when fishing for salmon a hook of stout and heavy pattern is often used, to which the delightful term "iron" is traditionally applied.

One of the great charms of fly-fishing (or any fishing for that matter) is the number of pet theories cherished by its practitioners: one of these is that a long shank makes it easier for the fish to lever the hook out. If you subscribe to this theory the answer would appear to be to use two shorter hooks tied in tandem. (See note on multiple-hook lures.)

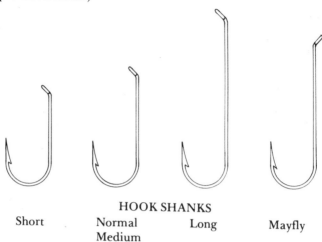

HOOK SHANKS

Short   Normal   Long   Mayfly
               Medium

While in some cases the original round section of the wire is retained, in others the hook is put through a press when the bend has been shaped so that the section becomes a vertical flat oval. Hooks treated in this way are described as "flat-forged" and the additional strength imparted by this process is well worth the trifling extra cost.

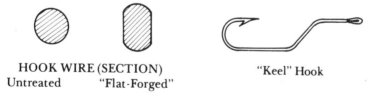

HOOK WIRE (SECTION)   "Keel" Hook
Untreated   "Flat-Forged"

In the "keel" hook, a comparatively recent invention by the American, Dick Pobst, the shank is bent into a "keel" so that the hook travels point uppermost thus (theoretically) avoiding getting caught up in weeds or snags. Some other theoreticians may say that its shape may affect its hooking capabilities.

It does however appear to have one very real advantage for the reservoir angler who has an unfortunate propensity for hitting the hook on the dam wall when making his back-cast. As the dressing is put on "upside down" it seems that most frequently it is the bend of the hook rather than the point that comes into contact with the concrete, thus considerably reducing the incidence of point breakage.

BENDS

Here again there is a wide variety of shapes to suit individual purposes, tastes and theories:

The "round" bend is self-explanatory; the curve of the bend is a steady and regular segment of a circle.

In the "Limerick" bend the curve starts fairly gently from the shank but is more accentuated towards the "bite".

The "Sproat" bend is best described as being a cross between the "round" and the "Limerick".

In the "sneck" bend the outer section of the curve has been flattened off to impart a somewhat square appearance.

| Round | Limerick | Sproat | Sneck |

GAPE

Hooks can be obtained in various proportional widths of "gape". Possibly the wide-gape hook affords a more secure hold on the fish, but some dressers prefer a narrower gape for the reason that when the body is put on there is not a big expanse of bend visible below the dressing.

POINTS AND BARBS

These can be cut or ground in various shapes; "straight", "hollow" or "Dublin".

The important thing is that the point should be sharp* and the barb not cut too deep. A hook with a short point and a shallow barb will obviously give quicker penetration and this pattern has the added advantage that it makes for easier and less damaging release of an undersized or out-of-season fish; it may also make it easier to lose a hooked fish while playing it but that is up to the man who is handling the rod!

The barb and point can be "flat", i.e. in the same horizontal

---

* One thing to beware of when considering points is that some hooks ("knife" point) carry a sharp edge between the tip of the point and the barb; if a fish is hooked in a soft part of the mouth this edge can soon cut a slit out of which the hook will fall.

plane as the rest of the hook, or bent outwards slightly.

Looked at from above, if the point is inclined to the right it is described as "kirbed" and if to the left as "reversed".

| Kirbed | Straight | Reversed |

Such offset points probably make for more sure hooking of a fish but some purists have yet another pet theory that they impart a slightly "corkscrew" motion to the fly and spoil its action.

Care must always be taken when placing such offset hooks in the fly-tying vice that only the straight part of the point is actually in the jaws of the vice or the pressure will cause the hook to snap at the bend.

Barbless hooks, where the cut barb is replaced by a double crank in the point, are being increasingly used; the beauty of these being that an undersized or out-of-season fish can easily and quickly be released without handling or damage. However, if you make a habit of using this type of hook you must remember to maintain tight contact with the fish or there is a good chance of its kicking free.

One final word on the subject of points: sharpness is important so when the tying of the fly is completed touch up the point with a fine-grade hone before putting it in the fly-box for use.

DOUBLE AND TREBLE HOOKS
While there are anglers who regard these with a measure of distaste they are nevertheless quite widely used.

In the "double" the wire is bent and brazed so as to provide two pointed and barbed legs set at an angle of about 120°. The "treble" has an additional leg brazed on to give three equally spaced points.

The "Esmond Drury" treble has a longer shank than usual, with the eye bent over to allow for the tying of a "Turle" or "Cairnton" knot. These trebles are very effective hookers.

With mounts such as the "Waddington" (p. 142) which carry a

treble one sometimes has the misfortune to break the point off one leg and would normally discard the lure. It is possible to salvage these by obtaining trebles in which one leg is left "open" and not brazed to the others, thus allowing a replacement hook to be "sprung" on to the mount. Hooks of such type are included in the range made by the Norwegian manufacturers, O. Mustad & Son of Oslo.

HOOK SCALES

The question of the scales of hook sizes is one that frequently confounds not only the beginner but also the more experienced tyer.

Many years ago the hook makers made an attempt to standardise hook sizes and brought out what was known as the "Old" or "Redditch" scale. This was based on the overall length of the hook (but some manufacturers excluded the eye while others included it!) and ranged from $1\frac{1}{4}$-inch for a size 1 down to $\frac{7}{32}$ inch for a size 18; in other words the larger the size number the smaller the hook.

In 1886 the "New" or "Pennell" scale was introduced. This had the same basis of linear measurement but the numbering was reversed, the scale number rising directly with the size of the hook. The two scales crossed or coincided at size 8. Needless to say this caused even more confusion and most manufacturers reverted to the "Old" scale.

More difficulty and confusion arises when one attempts to compare nominal sizes of hooks with differing widths of gape. The question of whether a round-bend hook with an average gape should bear the same size number as a round-bend of the same overall length but with a narrow gape, is one that could provide a topic of long and possibly heated discussion.

Fortunately as with most things there is a simple answer to this problem. Find a brand of hook that suits your taste and be guided by that manufacturer's own sizing, ignoring the "Old" and "New".

3

MANUFACTURED MATERIALS

TYING-SILK

While the hook is the skeleton of your fly, the tying-silk is the material which holds the whole thing together.

It is usually obtainable in two grades, the "Gossamer" (or very fine) which is used for almost all our work, and the slightly stouter "Naples" for the larger lures and for salmon flies.

Both grades are supplied in standard size reels in a wide variety of colours. This standard reel gives about 45 metres of the "Gossamer" grade.

These standard size reels are recommended in preference to buying larger spools; not only are most bobbin-holders designed to take the standard reel but silk can deteriorate with age and a "bulk" purchase could prove a false economy.

As regards colours, black and brown must be considered as essential, with olive, yellow, orange and red well up in the list of runners; other colours are not so likely to be needed and can be added as required. Whether or not it is something to do with the dyes used in the manufacturing process but it may be found that silk of certain colours will break more easily than others.

NYLON AND TERYLENE THREAD

Although some of the earlier forms of nylon were apt to be too "springy" or elastic for satisfactory tying, the modern threads, particularly Terylene, are excellent. Not only is there a wide range of shades but their strength as compared with natural silk enables one to use a finer grade.

As already mentioned, both silks and nylons may deteriorate if left exposed to light and air, so it is advisable to store them in a closed box preferably suitably partitioned. After use, the loose end of the thread should be secured in the notch cut in the flange of the spool, otherwise the spools have a happy knack of unwinding and getting well and truly mixed.

WAX

Waxing the thread before use serves two main purposes; first, to smooth down any "hairy" fibres that might project from the thread and secondly to cover the thread with a "tacky" coating to which fur, etc. will readily adhere when making "dubbed" bodies (see Chapter 6, page 63).

A piece of clear saddler's wax or ordinary hard beeswax about the size of a filbert nut will last for years.

Specially prepared waxes can be bought but generally speaking these are unnecessarily expensive and in the case of those in liquid form are often messy to use.

Many suppliers offer spools of ready-waxed thread, usually of American origin.

FLOSS SILK

This material, sometimes called "marabou" (not to be confused with the marabou feather from Turkeys), is widely used for making the bodies of flies and for certain "trimmings". As with the tying-silk it is supplied in standard-size reels in a wide range of colours. Black is the colour most frequently called for, with yellow and scarlet also popular; again, the range can be added to as necessary.

The usual type consists of two strands twisted together. One strand only is normally used in forming a body and details as to the use of this are given in Chapter 6, page 62.

The comments made on the storage of tying-silk apply with equal force to this material.

RAYON AND ACETATE FLOSS

Rayon, or Acetate floss is also available and the range of shades is even wider although some of the colours tend to be somewhat brash.

One advantage of acetate floss is that if the finished body is painted over with clear acetone or other suitable solvent it will fuse into a homogeneous covering.

These man-made fibres are also obtainable in *fluorescent* form which will add considerable "flash" and visibility to a fly. The colours tend to be even more garish and if you use too much of this material you are apt to produce something which is guaranteed to scare every self-respecting fish within half a mile!

CHENILLE

This material, used in the carpet and furnishing trades, consists of a core of thread into which is woven projecting fibres, usually of wool. Wound neatly round the shank of a hook it forms a quick and very effective body.

It is usually supplied in cut lengths of some five yards and bigger "bulk" spools are not easy to obtain.

TINSELS

These are used extensively for making attractive "flashy" bodies (see Chapter 6, page 68) and also for "ribbing" (also Chapter 6).

Flat tinsel is very thin metal foil cut to various widths and is usually sold in reels of about 10 yards. Silver and Gold in the narrow ($\cdot$015 inch or 0$\cdot$40 mm) and slightly wider ($\cdot$023 inch or 0$\cdot$60 mm) sizes are the only types which the dresser is likely to want. Other "metallic" colours are available but are very rarely called for.

An excellent substitute for metallic tinsel is the plastic material known as "Lurex", which can be obtained in large spools of some 75 yards from most drapery or needlework shops. It is easy stuff to work with and its only disadvantage is that the needlework spool material is very narrow.* It is also possible to buy sheets or strips which can be cut to the width required; this is best done by laying the strip on a flat sheet of glass and, using a metal straight-edge, cutting it with a razor-blade. Lurex has the added advantage that it does not tarnish like metallic tinsels, all of which should be kept in airtight containers when not in use.

If your tinsel has tarnished, draw it a few times through a piece of chamois-leather to polish and brighten it.

Some of the old traditional fully-dressed salmon-flies may call for the inclusion of "embossed" tinsel. This is merely flat tinsel which has been put through a machine to produce an embossed pattern on it.

For "ribbing" (see Chapter 6) a "round" or "oval" tinsel is often used, either gold or silver. This consists of a covering of very fine gauge wire wound over a silk core. It can be purchased in small spools of about ten yards or it can be obtained in larger quantities from some specialist embroidery shops.

WIRE

Many dressings call for a ribbing of gold wire, so the fly-dresser will want a reel of this in his kit. The usual size is about $\cdot$005 inch or 0$\cdot$12 mm.

Some soft copper wire of the same gauge or slightly heavier can also be included; this will be used to form the heavy underbody of a fly which one wants to sink fairly rapidly.

* Spools of double-width Lurex are now available from some suppliers of fly-tyer's materials.

Plate II

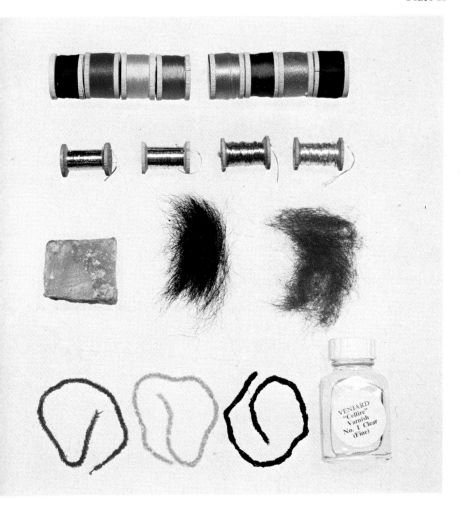

SOME MATERIALS USED IN FLY-DRESSING

Tying-silk.	Floss-silk.
Flat tinsel.	Round or oval tinsel (note silk "core").
Wax.	Dyed Seal's fur.
Strands of Chenille.	Clear varnish.

Plate III

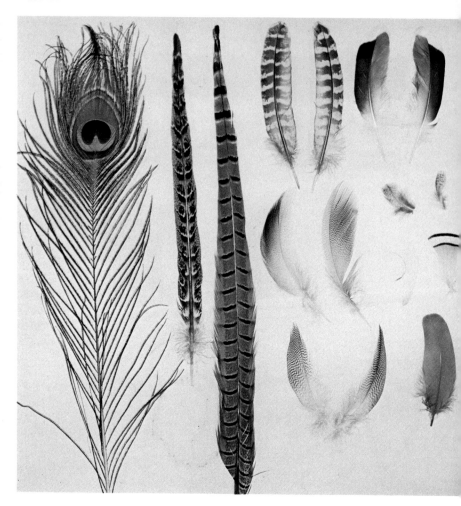

SOME FEATHERS USED IN FLY-DRESSING

Peacock tail.

Hen Pheasant
wing secondaries.

Mallard "blues"

Hen Pheasant Tail.

"Bronze" Mallard
shoulder.

English Partridg
neck.

Golden Pheasan
"tippet".

Cock Pheasant tail.

Teal shoulder.

Goose dyed scarl
(substitute
for Ibis).

Gold, silver and copper wire can be bought in small spools but again it is possible to get these from a wire-drawing firm in larger quantities at a cheaper rate.

As with tinsels the same precautions against tarnishing should be taken.

TUBING

The "skeleton" of a tube-fly is a short length of metal (brass for heavy flies, aluminium for light), hard nylon or plastic tube, the bore and wall-thickness varying according to the type of fly required.

Nylon or plastic can be cut with strong scissors but if metal tubing is to be used it will have to be cut with a fine-blade hacksaw. In this case you must remember to smooth down any rough edges that might cut or fray the leader.

Full details of how to make a tube-fly are given in Chapter 9.

VARNISH

This is used to finish off the fly, to seal the threads of the whip-finish at the head and to give it a nice shiny "insecty" appearance. The ordinary quick-drying "clear" cellulose varnish is in general use but polyurethane varnish, which is slightly slower in drying, gives a harder and stronger result.

Cellulose varnish evaporates very quickly and care should be taken not to leave the cap off the bottle unnecessarily. If it does go thick and treacly, it can be thinned down again by adding small amounts of acetate thinners which can be bought quite cheaply from most ironmonger's or model-maker's shops.

Spilt varnish, particularly the cellulose type, will cause extensive damage to furniture surfaces and carpets and it is a sensible precaution to stand the bottle in a properly shaped recess in a block of wood.

A frequent nuisance of varnish is that the cap of the bottle will seize-up. To avoid this, when you buy a new bottle wipe the threads of the bottle and of the cap clean and dry and then smear them very lightly with vaseline; this proves very effective. Always check that there are no "foreign bodies" such as bits of hair or feather either on the neck of the bottle or inside the cap. These will always assist the process of seizing-up.

As well as the clear variety, varnish in black, red and other colours is sometimes called for, usually for salmon-flies, but a touch of ordinary enamel paint of the appropriate colour will serve equally well.

4

NATURAL MATERIALS

Having dealt with "manufactured" materials, we now come to consider the natural materials, feathers and fur. (For further detail on this subject refer also too Chapter 12. "Collection of Materials".)

FEATHERS
These are traditional materials extensively used by the fly-dresser and in order to use them to their best effect it is essential to be fully conversant with their structure and characteristics.

HACKLES
Here I am going to claim the privilege of old age and digress for a moment. The newcomer to angling and to fly-fishing in particular will soon find that in this activity the same word may carry different meanings or shades of meaning only apparent from the context. Take for example the word "cast", which can mean the action of throwing or propelling a fly or bait, it can indicate the "leader" or length of gut or monofilament connecting the fly to the main line, or it can even refer to a plaster-of-paris model of a fish! "Hackle" is no exception; it may refer to that part of a fly which represents the legs of a struggling insect (see Chapter 5. "Parts of a Fly"), or it may mean a bird's neck feather which we use for this representation.

COCK HACKLES
For dry or floating flies one normally uses a hackle from the neck of a cockerel. As will be seen in the sketch opposite, these are narrow tapering feathers composed of a central stem or quill, carrying on each side a "web" of individual fibres lying closely alongside each other so as to present an almost "solid" appearance. At the base of the feather is a mass of fluffy fibre; this is known as "flue" and is discarded before the feather is used.

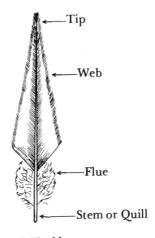

Cock Hackle

As one wants a dry fly to sit lightly on the surface of the water the individual fibres of a good quality cock hackle should be clean, stiff and springy and if the web is drawn through the fingers from the tip to the base those fibres should tend to resume their natural close "lay" immediately. The outer surface of the hackle (hereafter referred to as the bright side) should be glossy and bright in colour and the inner surface (the dull side) should be free from a chalky or brittle appearance.

As expanded in Chapter 12. (Collection of Materials.) the major problem nowadays is the increasing difficulty in obtaining really high-grade cock hackles.

This is possibly a suitable place to say something about the colours of hackles for which the various dressings may call, although whether such varieties will actually be obtainable is another matter.

Red
While this, if the context so indicates, can mean the colour of a pillar-box or a Guardsman's tunic, the term "red" mentioned in a dressing usually refers to the bright mahogany red of the neck of the old "Rhode Island Red" cockerel.

Dun

Another example of a word with two entirely different meanings. A "dun" can be an insect at one stage of its life-cycle, that when the pupa has hatched into a flying insect and before its final change or ecdysis into the perfect insect or imago. Colour-wise dun indicates a brown with a somewhat "smoky" appearance and there are many sub-shades of it:

"Blue dun" is a smoky blue-grey.

"Rusty dun" is a dull smoky brown with a redder or "rusty" edge.

"Honey dun" is a paler brown with a cream or honey coloured edge.

"Olive dun" is a smoky brown with a khaki or olive tinge.

Ginger

A light cinnamon brown.

White

A pure white is rare, the more usual being an off-white or pale cream.

Black

Here again the pure colour is uncommon; a "natural" black is usually tinged with a brown or rusty shade.

Iron-Blue

A blue-black "inky" colour.

Having mentioned most of the "self" colours, there are several bi-coloured varieties in common use.

Badger

A white or off-white hackle with a narrow black stripe next to the quill (this stripe is known as a "list"). These will be found on the neck of a "Light Sussex" bird.

Greenwell

A ginger hackle with a black list.

Furnace

A bright mahogany red with a black list.

Grizzle
A variegated hackle speckled or barred with black or some other dark colour on a paler background.

Coch-y-Bonddu
The nearest that the non-Welshman can get to the pronunciation of this is "cockabundy"! It is a mahogany red with a black list and black edges to the web.

Cree
Mottled bars of ginger and black, obtained by crossing the Rhode Island Red and Plymouth Rock breeds (if you can find them!).

*   *   *

At a pinch these bi-coloured hackles can be produced by the method advocated by Geoffrey Bucknall. Take a plain hackle of the appropriate base-colour, mask off with stiff paper the area to be left natural and colour the exposed portions with some indelible marking agent dabbed on with a felt-tipped pen.

It is usually cheaper, and certainly more convenient from the point of view of storage, to buy hackles in the form of a "cape". This is the complete skin of the cockerel's neck, duly dried and treated with preservative.

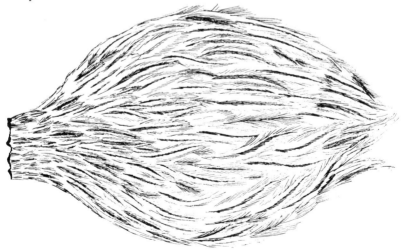

"Cape"

Domestic Cockerel

The small neat feathers towards the top of the neck are those required for the smaller sizes of flies, the longer hackles at the base of the cape being useful only for the larger "streamer" flies or for making "false" hackles (see page 84).

Other hackle feathers are also provided by our cockerel:

Spade hackles come from lower down the bird's body; these are shorter and more steeply tapered than the true neck hackles.

Saddle hackles are the long, generally brightly-coloured, feathers hanging down either side of the tail. Usually a good half of the feather consists of useless flue but the long tips (though often soft in texture) come in handy for streamer flies.

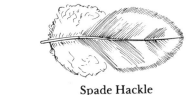

Spade Hackle

Saddle Hackle

HEN HACKLES

Hackles from the neck of a domestic hen are shorter than those of the cock and are not so tapered, having rounded ends or tips. The individual fibres making up the web are softer and more "feathery" than the hard clean fibres in the hackle of a cock bird.

These softer fibres move freely in the water and provide the action needed for a wet fly.

Hackles from other domestic poultry such as Guinea Fowl (Gallena) and those of game-birds such as Partridge and Grouse are generally shorter and rounder in shape, and in the case of wild birds carry a small fluffy feather at the base. The purpose of this is merely to keep the bird warm and it should be discarded with the "flue".

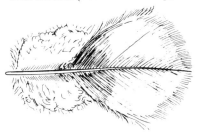

Hen Hackle (note rounded tip)

Partridge Hackle (enlarged)

WINGS

"Wing" is another instance of two shades of meaning for the same word. We use segments from the wing feather of a bird to make the wing of the fly, but just to add to the confusion we occasionally make a wing (of a fly) from a hackle (of a bird)!

If you examine the wing of a typical bird:

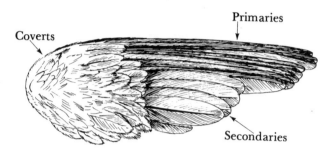

Bird Wing

you will notice that the long feathers on the upper or "leading" edge, called "primaries", have a comparatively narrow strip of web on one side of the quill, while on the other is a wider strip the section of which shows a double or "switchback" camber.

Generally speaking, these primaries are not so useful to the fly-dresser as the feathers from lower down the wing, the "secondaries". It will be seen that these have an almost equal width of web either side of the quill and, viewed in section, they show a regular even camber on both sides.

As with hackle feathers, wing feathers carry a certain amount of flue at their bases which has to be removed before the feather is used.

As elaborated in the notes on "Winging" (Chapter 8), to form the wing of a fly you usually need equal matching segments from a matched pair of right and left wing feathers.

An interesting (and useful) feature of the individual fibres forming the web is that if these are examined under a microscope it will be seen that each fibre is armed with minute hooks which engage with corresponding hooks on the next fibre like a "zip"-fastener. (The ornithologist refers to the individual fibres as "barbs" and the little hooks thereon as "barbules". For the sake of avoiding possible confusion with the "barb" of the fish-hook I shall continue to refer to these as individual web fibres.)

If such fibres are parted they can be stroked together again and will resume their former united and smooth appearance. It is even possible to join in this way two or more segments from different wings to form a composite or "married" segment. (See Chapter 8, "Winging".)

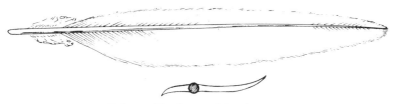

Primary Feather and Section

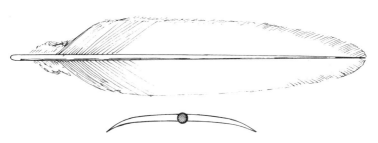

Secondary Feather and Section

TAIL FEATHERS

These often resemble wing secondaries and can be used in much the same way.

In the case of some tail feathers the "zip-fastener" effect of the individual web fibres has become rudimentary or has disappeared completely with the result that the fibres appear as separate entities. An extreme example of this is the feathery fronds down the quill of a Peacock tail.

Larger individual fibres of wing or tail feathers are referred to as "herls".

ANIMAL FUR AND HAIR

Having thus plucked the unfortunate fowl we now turn our attention to animals, the fur and hair of which is widely used in modern fly-dressing. The dense undercoat or short fur such as that of the Mole is used for making "dubbed" bodies (see Chapter 6), and the longer individual hairs, known as "guard" hairs, are used in place of feather fibres for making wings and in some cases hackles.

While various types of animal hair are listed in Chapter 12 (Collection of Materials), special mention ought to be made here of Seal's fur. This is short "springy" fur from the young Arctic Seal and can be purchased from any supplier of fly-tying materials. Not only does this have water-resistant properties but it has a nice sparkling appearance. In its natural state it is a dirty cream in colour but fortunately it takes dye well and is obtainable in a wide range of colours.

Under this heading we can include wool and mohair which again are available in any shade required. Wool can also be obtained dyed in various "fluorescent" colours.

For some notes on the storage of feathers and fur see Chapter 13.

*   *   *

Various other materials both natural and man-made such as raffia or bast, cork, polythene etc. will in due course find their way into the materials cabinet. These will be dealt with in more detail as they crop up later in the book.

Some people will even go to the length of adorning the heads of flies (or rather, lures) with a pair of metal or glass beads to represent "eyes". My own feeling is that the proper place for such horrors is on someone else's plug-bait!

PART II

FLY-DRESSING PROCESSES AND TECHNIQUES

5

BASIC FLY-DRESSING PROCEDURES

To make a success of fly-tying it is vitally important to understand and master the basic procedures which go to the building up of the finished fly from the bare hook. Later chapters will deal with the processes in detail.

As many of the flies with which you will come into contact are deliberate imitations of a natural insect it will help if you have a basic knowledge of the types of insect which are likely to be encountered, and this is possibly an appropriate place to add some notes about them.

In tying such imitations of the "natural" one naturally wishes to achieve a result which bears as close a resemblance as possible to the insect in question and this end will be better served if the dresser is conversant with its life-cycle and habits.

The insect branch of the animal kingdom covers an infinite number of different species, but as the student will learn from the books on the subject mentioned in Chapter 14 there are three main

43

"Orders" which are of interest to the fish and therefore to the fisherman:

Ephemeroptera, or up-winged flies, e.g. Mayflies, Olives and Caenis.

Diptera, or flat-winged flies, e.g. Cowdung Flies, Mosquitoes and Chironomids.

"Roof" effect from head on

Trichoptera, or those with "roof" shaped wings, the Sedges or Caddis Flies.

(Note: The word "sedge" to the fly-fisherman very rarely relates to the coarse grass-like plant growing by the waterside; it is nearly always used to describe the Caddis insect!)

The life-cycle involves several radical changes in appearance. From the *egg* hatches a swimming or crawling creature rather like a maggot, the *larva*. When this has reached a certain stage of development the skin is split and shed (a process known as *Ecdysis*) and from this emerges the *pupa* (the equivalent of the chrysalis of the butterfly or moth). Further growth and development takes place and again the skin is shed to release a winged insect, the *dun* or *sub-imago*. This may again undergo a further ecdysis to complete the cycle with the perfect insect, the *imago* or *spinner* (yet another example of two different meanings for the same word; to some anglers a spinner is a lump of wood, plastic or metal liberally festooned with treble hooks, which is drawn through the water to attract a predatory fish). When mating and egg-laying (or ovipositing, if you wish to appear technical) has been completed the exhausted insect falls on the water as a *"spent"* spinner.

Often the time spent in these various stages may vary quite considerably, and some insects spend several months in the larval stage and only a matter of hours as a flying creature.

Some species may omit or combine certain of these stages.

The insect in the swimming or crawling stage is referred to as a *"nymph"* and it is at this stage that it is particularly vulnerable to the appetite of a hungry fish.

It is as well to remember, when attempting to tie imitations of the natural insect, that the "natural" usually has a dainty and translucent appearance. The effect of the imitation will be minimal if the dressing is too heavy and "solid".

THE COMPONENT PARTS OF A FLY OR LURE

Before starting on practical work, the beginner should be fully conversant with the features that make up the fly and the terms applied to those various parts.

We start with the *bare hook*.

Some patterns have a *tail* which is tied in at the rear end above the shank.

The shank is now covered with silk, tinsel, fur etc. to form the *body*.

This may be bound spirally with tinsel or wire to give a segmented or "transparent" appearance or to provide an element of flash; this is known as "*ribbing*".

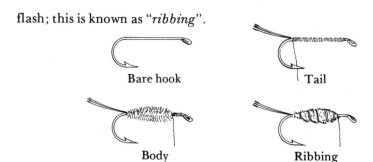

Bare hook   Tail

Body   Ribbing

Next comes the *hackle*, to represent the legs of a struggling insect. This may take various forms:

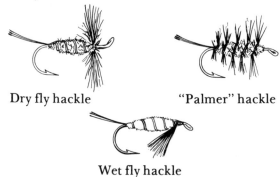

Dry fly hackle   "Palmer" hackle

Wet fly hackle

Then we have the *wing*, which again can be of several types:

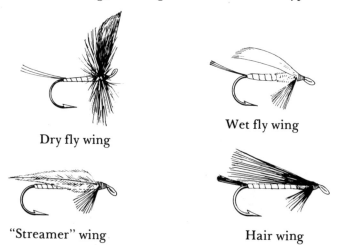

Dry fly wing

Wet fly wing

"Streamer" wing   Hair wing

Finally we have the *head*, formed of several neatly wound turns of tying-silk, secured with a "whip-finish" (see page 54) and then varnished.

The old traditional salmon-fly often had certain additional bits and pieces and these are set out in detail in the Chapter on salmon-flies.

DRESSING A FLY

Starting, "positioning" of material, finishing off and dealing with interruptions are the processes which are the firm basis on which all good fly-dressing is established and they must be fully mastered if proficiency is to be attained. Quite apart from the aesthetic satisfaction to the dresser of a fly neatly made and securely finished, that fly will surely fish more efficiently.

STARTING

First, check that your table or desk is well situated as regards light, that it and your chair are the proper comfortable height for working, and that the working-surface is firm and level. Nothing is more irritating than the slight slope down which tools and other things roll just as they are most wanted.

Secondly, see that you yourself are comfortable and that your hands are clean and dry. Check also that the tips of the fingers, particularly of the thumb and forefinger of both hands, are smooth and free from any little projecting bits of hard skin; these seem to act like a magnet to tying-silk and will snag it every time. If necessary rub these down with a manicure sand-board; the striker panel of a box of non-safety matches can be used for this if nothing else is available.

Place your background cloth of white plastic or "American Cloth" about one foot square along the edge of the working surface and erect the vice on it. Adjust the height of the column of the vice as necessary.

Spread out your tools in a shallow tray or container so that you do not have to go searching for anything once you have started and also set out in logical order in the recommended partitioned box all the materials you are going to need for the session's work. You want to avoid having to get up from your seat to go looking for a missing item once you have got into the "swing" of things.

If you propose to use a magnifier or enlarging spectacles get these into position.

Place a reel of tying-silk in the lugs of your bobbin-holder, draw off a few inches of silk and thread this through the aperture of the holder. (If you have difficulty in threading the silk either lick the end of it or give it a few quick strokes with the wax to give it a stiff clean end.) See that the silk is not twisted round one leg of the holder.

If you do not use a bobbin-holder cut off about a foot of tying-silk.

You are now all ready to start.

Select a fairly large hook, say a size 8 (Old or Redditch scale, see page 29); it is easier to start with a hook big enough for you to see clearly what goes on, and then to progress to the smaller sizes.

Place the hook in the jaws of the vice and clamp it when the point and barb are just "masked" by the jaws. If you leave any part of the point exposed it will surely catch the tying-silk and break it.

If you are using a hook with an "offcast" point, only the straight part of the point should be put in the vice; if you attempt to compress the offcast bend the hook will fracture.

Check that the shank of the hook slopes slightly above the horizontal; this will help to avoid the silk tending to run down into

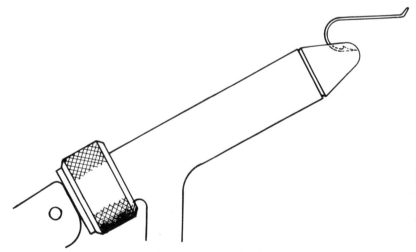

Hook clamped in vice
Note point masked and shank sloping slightly upwards

Plate IV

SOME TROUT FLIES AND LURES

Top Row

ck and Peacock Spider.   Dry "Greenwell's Glory".   Hairwing "Sweeney Todd".
Wet "March Brown".   "Invicta".

Middle Row

nged dry "Iron blue".   "Footballer".   Pheasant-tail nymph.   "Butcher".
"Cinnamon Sedge".

Bottom Row

"Muddler Minnow".   Badger "Matuka".   Mayfly.

Plate V

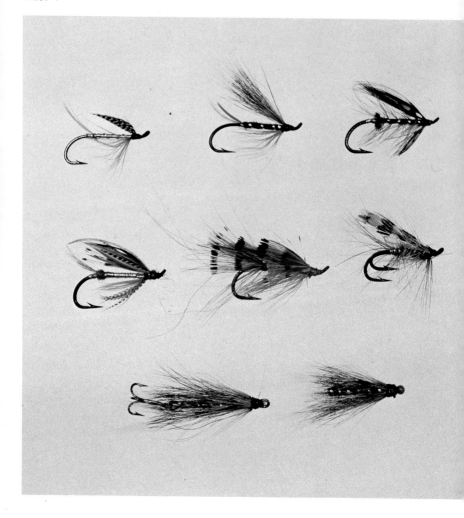

PATTERNS OF SALMON FLIES

Top Row

Low-water "Silver Blue".   Hairwing "Hairy Mary".   "Thunder and Lightnin

Middle Row

"Silver Doctor".   "General Practitioner".   Usk Grub.

Bottom Row

"Waddington". "Hairy Mary".   Tube-fly. "Hairy Mary".

the eye, a very common fault even among experienced dressers who should know better!

Test the hook for a firm hold in the vice by flicking the eye with a fingernail. This should give a resonant "ping" if the hook is of sound temper and firmly held. Few things are more irritating than the hook which slips in the jaws of the vice at the wrong moment.

"RUNNING-ON" THE TYING-SILK

Now take the loaded bobbin-holder (or the length of silk) and holding the spare end of the silk towards you with the left hand pass the bobbin-holder with the right hand across and above the shank at the throat. Always leave a space between the start of the eye and where the silk winding commences. Holding the end of the silk taut pass the bobbin-holder round the shank in a clockwise direction

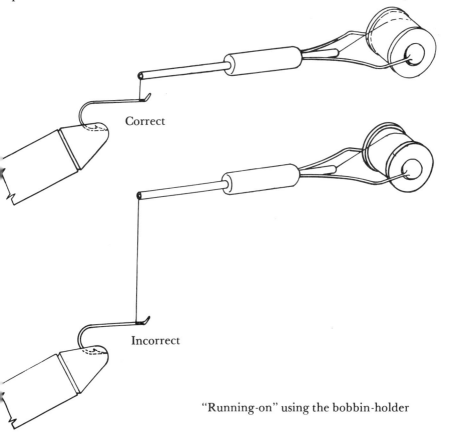

Correct

Incorrect

"Running-on" using the bobbin-holder

and bring it up again, thus "trapping" the loose end against the shank.

Keeping the silk taut, lay on the next turn immediately to the left of the first turn, tight up against it but not crossing it.

Touching turns like this will be referred to as "close-butting" turns.

If once the end of the silk has been securely trapped you hold the end taut and pointing to the rear of the hook at an angle of about 30° from the shank you will find that the next turn of silk will slide down automatically against the last turn and "close-butt" accordingly.

If you are careful to keep the fingers close to the hook allowing not more than a ½-inch of silk between the aperture of the bobbin-holder and the shank of the hook and to maintain even tension on the silk as you wind it you are less likely to form loose loops of silk which may allow the dressing to slip and spoil the work. See diagram.

About four or five turns from where you want to finish winding (usually at a place on the shank opposite the point of the hook) trim off the loose end, either by giving it a sharp upward flick which will break it off cleanly flush with the last turn or (if you lack the necessary confidence) by cutting it with scissors or a razor-blade, in which case you may leave a projecting whisker. This does not matter as you can cover it with the final turns.

You have now covered the shank with one evenly wound layer of tying-silk as a smooth foundation for whatever you wish to do next.

If you now wind the silk back in close-butting turns to your starting-point near the eye you will have covered the shank with a smooth double-thickness layer of silk which in itself would form a sufficient body for many flies.

Even though it may not be necessary for certain bodies (those where any irregularity in the primary winding will be covered over by the subsequent dressing), practise this "close-butting" winding until it becomes second nature.

"POSITIONING" AND TYING-IN MATERIAL

"Positioning" is a horrible word which will offend those who appreciate good English but I can think of no better term to describe the process of setting material in its proper position and holding it there while it is tied in and secured. It applies particularly to tails, wings and "false" hackles and the procedure will be repeated in the chapters dealing with those items.

If the material is placed properly in position on the hook at the beginning of the tying operation the rest is easy but unless this is carefully done the result will almost certainly be misshapen or out of proportion.

Remember first that it is very difficult to tie anything direct on to a bare metal shank, so always check that there is a "bed" of smooth turns of silk at the appropriate place on which to tie your material.

Pick up the material (e.g. a bunch of hackle fibres for a tail or slips of feather for a wing) by the butt or base with the thumb and forefinger of the right hand. Place this on top of the shank where you want it to be tied in and, as a carpenter does when fitting a piece of wood into a structure, "offer it up" or check it for length and size. If too long or too short, take hold of the tips of the bunch of material (i.e. the other end) with the left thumb and forefinger, move those of the right hand the required space and take hold with the right thumb and forefinger again. Release the left hand.

Offer it up again with the right hand (thumb towards you) and if the siting is now satisfactory open the grip of the underside of the thumb and finger slightly so as to enable them to embrace the actual shank of the hook. This should prevent the material moving as you carry out the next step.

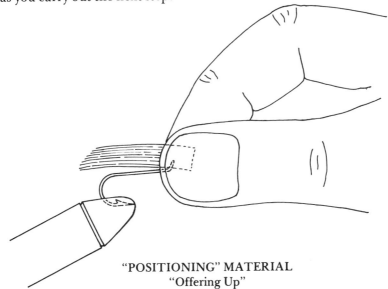

"POSITIONING" MATERIAL
"Offering Up"

With the left thumb and finger (thumb towards you) take hold first of the shank and then extend the grip to take in the bunch of material. The tips of the thumbs and forefingers of the opposite hands should now be touching each other.

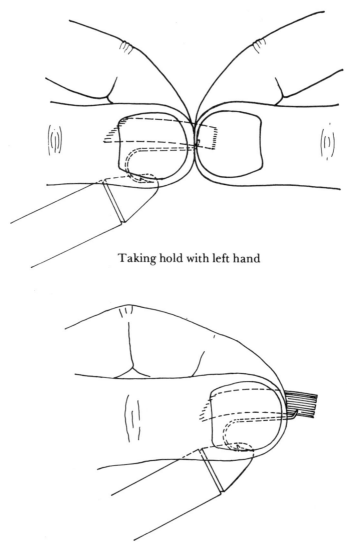

Taking hold with left hand

Material ready for tying in

Release the hold with the right hand, and the material should be firmly held in position in the right place by the left thumb and finger without having moved up, down or round the shank. It is thus ready for you to manipulate the tying-silk and to tie it in with the right hand.

Such "positioning" becomes almost automatic once it has been thoroughly practised.

A useful exercise to practise is to "roll" the tips of the thumb and forefinger together, both in the vertical and horizontal planes.

TYING-IN

Holding the material firmly thus, bring the working end of the silk up with the right hand, bringing it between the "home" side of the bunch of material you wish to tie in and the inside of the tip of the left thumb. Nip the silk between the tips of the left thumb and forefinger and pass it away from you over and down between the material and the inside of the tip of the left forefinger (i.e. on the "away" side). Hold the material firm and straight with the left hand as with the right you draw the silk vertically downwards steadily and firmly.

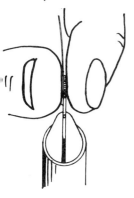 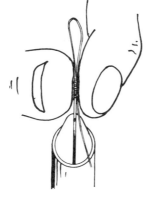 

TYING-IN

| Tying-silk taken upwards and nipped in position | Silk looped over and held again | Tying silk drawn down |

This applies to fixed components of the fly such as the tail or wing. Tying-in material which is later to be wound round the shank, e.g. for a body or a hackle, is a somewhat different procedure which is detailed in the appropriate chapters but the same basic requirement applies; the material must be held firmly in position as it is tied in.

FINISHING-OFF

While you can finish and secure the fly by tying a series of half-hitches it makes for a more secure and certainly neater and more professional finish if you tie what is known as a "whip-finish".

This can be done with the aid of a special tool designed for the purpose (Messrs. Veniards' model is illustrated below). Instructions for use are issued with each instrument.

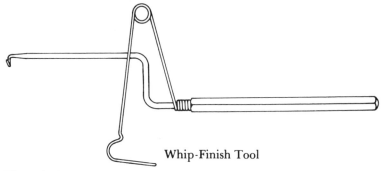

Whip-Finish Tool

The whole process of tying a whip-finish can be accomplished very easily and quickly with the fingers once the drill has been mastered:

Take hold of the running end of the silk with your right hand about six inches from the hook and keep it taut, leaving the remainder dangling down below your right hand.

Pick up the dangling bobbin-holder or spare end of silk with your left hand and pass it to your left anti-clockwise so that the spare end of the silk lies close along the shank, pointing to the rear and hard up against and on your side of the silk which you are holding taut with your right hand.

Bring this taut silk up with your right hand and take a clockwise turn round the neck of the hook trapping the loose end. Now take three or four further close-butting turns forward, winding not too tight.

Keeping the end of the length of silk or the bobbin-holder in the left hand take a firm but not too tight grip with the thumb and forefinger of the right hand of the turns which have just been laid on.

Now draw the loose end steadily towards the rear of the hook with the left hand in order to take up the loop or bight at the head of the hook. As soon as the silk starts to move, slacken very slightly the hold with the right hand and with the dubbing-needle or the nose of a pair of scissors keep the loop reasonably taut so as to stop the silk twisting or kinking as it is drawn tight. Trim off any waste silk as close to the head as possible.

It is a good idea to practise this "running-on" and "whip-finish" on a big sea-fishing hook set in a vice with jaws wide enough to hold it securely, using a piece of thin string or fishing line in place of the silk, then try with silk on a size 6 or 8 hook and finally on smaller sizes until you are fully conversant with it.

The whip-finish is illustrated in detail in the following photographs.

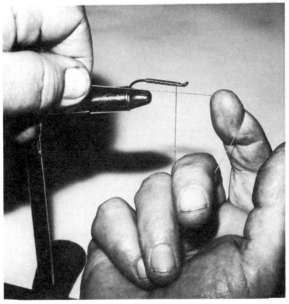

THE WHIP-FINISH (BY HAND)
1. Loop formed and held by fingers of right hand

THE WHIP-FINISH

2. Running end
   being "trapped"
   against shank

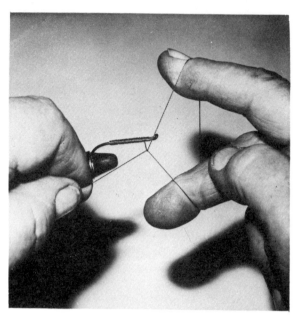

3. Bight being
   drawn closed

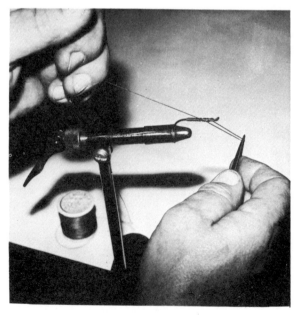

THE WHIP-FINISH (ALTERNATIVES)

1. Loop of different coloured silk positioned above shank

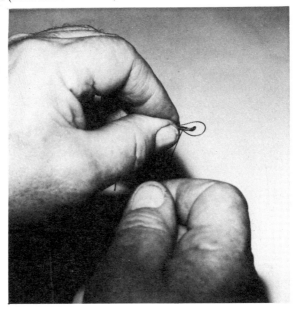

2. Loop whipped on and spare end of dressing silk being passed through. Note left forefinger holding whipping in position

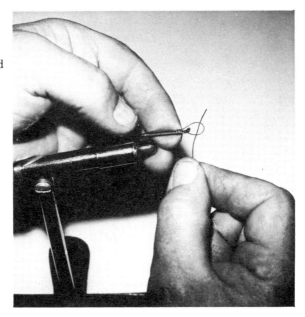

For the benefit of those who experience difficulty in tying a whip-finish, either with the fingers or by using the special tool, there is another method by which it can be done. This closely resembles the way in which one finishes off whipping a guide-ring on a fishing rod.

When you have wound the head of the fly and are ready to finish off, take another piece of silk about nine inches long, preferably of a contrasting colour. Double this and lay it on top of the head of the fly with the two ends pointing to the rear leaving a loop at the front.

Bind in this loop with three or four forward turns of silk, hold it with the thumb and forefinger of the left hand, then cut off the "working" end of your whipping silk to leave a loose end of about an inch or so. Pass this loose end through the loop and hold it fairly taut.

Now pick up both the loose ends of the odd silk forming the loop and draw these steadily to the rear. This will pull the loose end of the working silk back through the whipping, whereupon it should be drawn tight and trimmed off.

Do not attempt to tie a complete fly until you are fully conversant with these basic processes; they are the foundations of all good fly-dressing.

INTERRUPTIONS
If you are halfway through tying a fly and the lady of the house says that she wants you to clear the table so that she can lay it for supper don't say "Just a minute, dear," and then keep her waiting ten minutes while you finish what you are doing. There is a simple method of fastening off your work at any stage which will cope with this or any similar situation.

All you have to do is to make a loop in the running end of the tying silk underneath the shank, twist this loop a half-turn and pass it over the eye of the hook and down the shank to the exact point where you wish to fasten temporarily. Draw the loop tight and your work is secured with a half-hitch. You can then dismount your vice from the table, if necessary removing the fly with the bobbin-holder or loose silk attached.

Having done the washing-up or whatever other duty has been called for, re-erect the vice, replace the hook in its jaws, and carry on from where you left off. By such co-operation and by refraining from leaving rubbish for others to clear up, domestic acrimony and resistance to one's fly-tying activities can be avoided.

BREAKAGE

An involuntary interruption may occur when the tying-silk breaks, either from the application of too much tension or a fault in the silk. You may however be able to salvage your efforts and avoid the necessity of starting all over again.

The important thing is to grab the broken end of the silk with the fingers as quickly as possible to prevent its unravelling or slackening its hold on the materials already tied in. Then clip the larger pair of hackle-pliers on to this broken end and let it hang down taut.

At the point on the shank where the break occurred tie in a few fresh turns of silk (just as you did when starting originally) to trap and secure the broken end. Trim off the waste ends, both of the original broken thread and of the new tie, and carry on; nine times out of ten you will get away with it!

*   *   *

Before starting to tie flies in earnest, let me raise one final point.

After a short period of time you may find that there is a temptation to try anything once, to experiment and to tie several different patterns of fly at one session.

While this is all very laudable and understandable you will find that the results will be better if instead you tie at each sitting a number of flies of the same variety and size. Quite apart from the saving of time in selecting materials the standard of finish will improve with every one that comes off the production line. A certain stage in the dressing of a particular fly may call for some special skill and it is the repeated practice of this that makes for perfection.

Having acquired familiarity with the feel of the tools and the necessary degree of tension to be applied to the tying-silk when dealing with tying-in materials we will now deal in detail with the various processes involved in building up the different parts of the fly.

If each of these processes is thoroughly learned, any fly mentioned in any book can be tied once you know the components of the dressing.

6

BODIES, RIBBING AND TAILS

BODIES

This is a suitable place to remind the dresser always to allow himself
plenty of room between the eye of the hook and the front end of the
body. To "crowd" the eye is the commonest fault of all and a
frequent primary cause of this is that the shank of the hook when
placed in the vice points slightly downwards. Always give the shank
a slight upward slant.

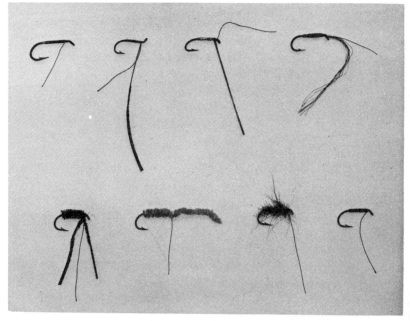

TYPES OF BODY DRESSING

Top: Plain Tying Silk   Stripped Peacock Quill   Flat Tinsel   Floss-Silk*
Lower: Peacock Herl   Chenille   Seals Fur   Floss Body Ribbed
* This is the modern Floss-Silk which does not fray out so well as the old variety.

Let us deal first with those types of body which do not require as an underbody the meticulous close-butting turns of tying-silk. These are bodies which in the course of formation will fill up and hide any unevenness in the foundation.

HERL

Herl from a Peacock tail makes an attractive natural looking body with a fat and hairy appearance.

Starting just behind the eye, run on the silk to a place on the shank opposite the hook-point and leave it hanging down, weighted either by the bobbin-holder or the bigger pair of hackle-pliers.

Take hold of the herl (using one or more strands according to the thickness of body required) with the left hand about half an inch from the base and place the root of the herl immediately under the shank of the hook and to the right of (and hard up against) the hanging end of silk. These roots should point slightly upwards and forwards.

Holding the herl very firmly with the left hand, bring the silk up with the right (keeping it taut) and wind it over the shank, trapping in the base of the herl.

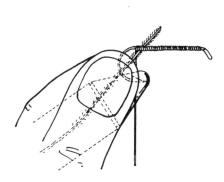

This is a clear example of what is meant by "tying-in" material. It is absolutely essential that the material which you are tying-in in this way is held rigid with the left hand as you trap it with the right.

If it is not held rigid it will nearly always roll away from you round the shank, as it also will if you allow too big a distance between the hand and the shank.

Having safely trapped the herl run on a couple more close-butted turns of silk to secure it, then wind the silk back to your starting point at the front end, again leaving the silk hanging down under tension. These turns of silk will bind the short ends of the herl down flush with the shank.

Grasp the loose end of the herl with the right hand, using either the fingers or the hackle-pliers, and wind it clockwise round and round the shank in neat close turns until the hanging end of the silk is reached. If you keep the hands close to the hook as you do this you will be less likely to make loose or "gappy" turns.

Holding the end of the herl with the right hand, very taut and pointing slightly forwards, pick up the silk with the left and keeping it taut bring it up and over to trap the herl again. Lay on a couple more close turns of silk to make sure that the herl is held securely and will not slip or unravel and then trim off the waste end of herl close up against the body. A sharp flick with the fingers will usually break this off cleanly.

If a more bulky body is required, tie in a bunch of several herls and twist or plait them together before winding them on as before. An alternative method is to leave the silk hanging at the rear end of the shank after tying in the bunch of herls, then twist the herls round the silk several times, and then wind on the silk and the herls together. This will help to obviate the body coming unwound if a herl gets severed by the teeth of the trout you catch on it!

Finer herls, such as those from the tail of a cock Pheasant, are used in much the same way but in these cases it will be advisable to use hackle-pliers to handle them.

There is a point to watch which applies here as well as elsewhere. When the silk is left hanging under tension there is a tendency for the weighting bobbin-holder or hackle-pliers to spin, causing the silk to untwist and weaken. Adjust the direction of the head of the vice so that the holder or pliers rest against the edge of the bench.

FLOSS-SILK

This material makes neat and attractive bodies, one of its main advantages being the wide range of colours available.

As in the last example, run on the tying-silk as far as the bend of the hook; again there is no need for close-butting turns. Leave the silk hanging, weighted as before.

Cut off a piece of floss-silk about nine inches long. As already mentioned in Chapter 3, this material usually consists of two strands twisted together. Untwist them and separate the strands; then take one strand and draw it several times between the fingers. This will straighten out the twist and leave a flat "ribbon" rather than a round "cord". Hold one end of this ribbon with the left hand and place it under the shank up against the tying-silk, just as you did with the herl, and hold it firmly as you trap it in.

You may find this operation easier if you give the end of the floss a lick before positioning it for tying-in.

Run the tying-silk back to the front end of the body, again binding down the short end of the floss, and leave it hanging under tension as before.

A loosely wound floss-silk body looks horrible so again keep the hands close to the hook and keep the floss taut as you wind it up the shank in a neat flat ribbon. To get a thicker body carry on winding the floss backwards and forwards up and down the shank; in this way you can build up a body either tapered at each end like a cigar or thicker at one end like a carrot. Finish winding at the place where the tying-silk is hanging down.

Holding the end of the floss very taut and slightly forwards with the right hand trap it with the tying-silk with the left, whip on a couple more turns to secure it and trim off the waste end of floss as near the shank as possible. You will have to cut this; floss-silk is strong stuff and you cannot flick it off as you did the herl.

You may find that some of the floss-silk manufactured nowadays appears to be composed of individual hard threads twisted together rather than the desirable soft fibrous material. This may require repeated drawing through the fingers to soften and flatten it.

DUBBED BODIES

To "dub" means to dress or cover, and to the fly-dresser it indicates covering the tying-silk with a coating of fur or similar fibres.

In order to make this covering adhere to the silk it is advisable to render the silk sticky or "tacky" and the best way of doing this is to wax it.

Pull off about nine inches of silk from the reel or bobbin-holder; hold the lump of wax in the closed palm of the left hand for a few minutes to warm and soften the surface, then draw the silk several times across it, pressing the silk on the wax with the left thumb.

The silk must be drawn quickly and lightly; it is essential that it moves fast so that the friction melts the wax and deposits an even coating on the silk. If you hold it too hard or pull it slowly the silk will stick and break every time.

Having done this, wipe the fingers dry and clean on the piece of rag or cloth that you should have ready and wind the silk down the shank of the hook as before.

If it is desired to leave waxing the silk until a later stage in the proceedings or if it is found that the previous application was insufficient, again warm the wax, then holding the silk very taut with one hand give it several short quick downward rubs or strokes with the other. Be very careful to keep these strokes quick and light; a slow movement will always break the silk. Don't forget to wipe the fingers again.

Have ready a tin-lid or other shallow container to take the fur you propose to use to cover the silk. Fur for dubbing, e.g. Mole or Hare, is usually kept "on skin", i.e. a small piece of the dried or cured skin of the animal with the coat still on it. Pluck off a few pinches of fur with the nails of the thumb and finger. Place these on the receptacle and "tease" the fibres thoroughly apart with the point of a needle to separate them so that there are no "lumps" of fur.

Holding the waxed silk very taut with the left hand, with the thumb and second finger of the right pick up a small pinch of the teased-out fibres and "twiddle" or roll on to the taut silk with a clockwise movement.

Press hard with the thumb and finger as you roll it but remember to release the pressure at the end of the roll or you will unravel it again, particularly if you have omitted to clean all the wax off your fingers.

Repeat this with successive pinches of fur until a length of about an inch or so of the silk is covered with a thin even "sausage" of fur, the top end of which should of course be as near to the shank as possible.

Keeping the silk well taut, wind this sausage of fur fibres in even turns up the shank to produce a body of the shape and thickness required. When sufficient body material has been wound on, keep the silk taut at the front end of the body with one hand and nip off any excess fur with the fingernails of the other. A couple of turns of "clean" silk and the body is complete.

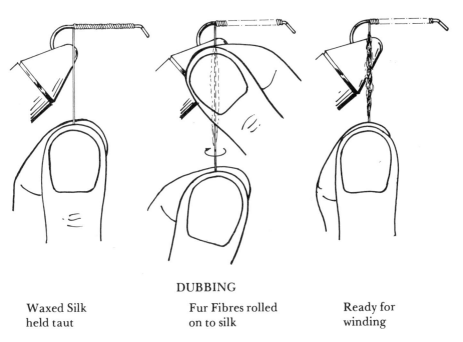

DUBBING

Waxed Silk held taut	Fur Fibres rolled on to silk	Ready for winding

A material very widely used by fly-dressers for dubbed bodies is Seal's fur, either left natural or dyed in a variety of colours, and this is usually supplied in packets of cut fibres. This fibre is very springy and while this characteristic imparts a nice bristly appearance to the fly it is apt to make it difficult stuff to dub; it tends to spring away from the silk as soon as it is rolled on.

Dubbing with Seal's fur can be rendered easier by adding to it a small amount of sheep's wool of the same colour; cut off about half an inch, tease this out very thoroughly with the needle into its individual fibres or "nap" and mix it well with the Seal's fur before applying it to the silk. A good way of mixing it is to make a "sandwich" of fur and wool and keep pulling it apart until thoroughly blended.

A general point to remember when dealing with dubbed bodies is that when the body material gets wet there is a tendency for the colour of the tying-silk to show through: it is sometimes worth the trouble of selecting a lighter shade of silk.

The following are some other body materials:

Wool

An effective body can be made from wool either by tying-in a single strand and winding it as you did the herl or, to give a rougher and less solid appearance, by teasing out the fibres and dubbing it on the silk. Waxing the silk is unnecessary as wool will adhere to it readily without assistance.

Mohair

This is Goat hair which usually comes in the form of long strands and is best used in a similar way to floss-silk.

Raffia or Bast

This makes very realistic bodies for Mayflies. Wet the raffia, draw it through the fingers to smooth it out, split it into a strip about $\frac{1}{8}$-inch wide and wind it on in a neat flat ribbon until the required shape of body is obtained.

The thorough wetting before use is important; the raffia will tighten up as it dries and when completely dry should be given a coat of clear varnish to waterproof it and to prevent it slackening again.

Cork

Cork used as an underbody makes a fly which is virtually unsinkable. Cover the shank with a layer of tying-silk and then smear both top and bottom surfaces with a quick-drying adhesive (clear "Bostik" is excellent).

Find a wine-bottle cork of good quality with nice close grain and with a razor-blade cut out a short strip about $\frac{1}{8}$-inch square. Trim this to the shape required, slit it lengthwise to about half its depth, open the slit and push the cork into position over the shank. Wind the silk tightly criss-cross backwards and forwards over the cork and allow the adhesive to dry before covering it with whatever body material is desired.

Alternatively, cut a paper-thin strip of cork and roll this round the shank, securing it with adhesive.

Foam Rubber, etc.

This and other man-made materials such as Polystyrene foam can also be used for bodies. These materials are easily trimmed to shape with a razor-blade or scissors.

None of the foregoing types of body has necessitated a foundation of close-butting turns of tying-silk but in the cases of those that now follow it is essential that the underbody is perfectly even and smooth if the final result is to have the proper neat appearance.

Quill

Quill is one of the traditional "natural" body materials. While occasionally the stripped quill or stem of a hackle feather is used, the more common material for this purpose is the quill of a Peacock herl, possibly dyed to the required shade.

To strip the fluffy fibre from a Peacock herl in order to leave a nice clean quill, hold the herl in one hand and with the nails of the thumb and finger of the other strip off the fibre, doing only about a quarter of an inch at a time, until you have about an inch and a half of clean quill free from "whiskers".

An alternative (and possibly easier) method of doing this is to hold the herl on a flat surface and remove the fibre with firm strokes with an ordinary pencil-rubber.

Wind the tying-silk in close-butting turns to the bend of the hook, then tie in the butt of the quill just as you did with the untreated herl, again remembering to hold it very firmly as you tie it in.

Wind the silk back to the front end again in close-butting turns and leave it hanging there under tension. Now take hold of the quill with the right hand and wind it clockwise in close turns, without gaps or overlapping, up to the silk.

Secure it with the silk as before, trim off the waste end of quill and you should have a neat smooth body with a striped or segmented appearance similar to that of an insect.

Bodies made from the stripped quill of a hackle feather give a somewhat "beaded" appearance which is equally attractive.

Horsehair

This is applied in a manner very similar to that for the last item.

It should be remembered that horsehair is very hard and slippery stuff and requires extra care in securing it both where it is tied in and where it is finished off. It is advisable therefore to smear the silk underbody with adhesive and then when the horsehair has been wound up as far as the silk it should be secured with a couple of tight turns of silk; then fold the hair back over those turns and whip two more turns of silk over this fold towards the rear.

To get a striped or "football jersey" effect tie in at the same time two strands of horsehair of different colours and wind them on together, being careful not to let them cross.

Tinsel

A nice smooth flat tinsel body with no apparent "seams" is one of the hall-marks of a good fly-dresser.

Once the tinsel is tied in properly there is no difficulty in winding it up the body in butting but not overlapping turns provided, and this is essential, that there is a smooth and level underbody of tying-silk.

Unless however the tinsel is neatly tied in to start with there is apt to be a "lump" where it was tied in and if this lump appears at the tail of the fly it can ruin the appearance of it.

My own view is that the following method of tying a tinsel body produces the best results. Admittedly it means using a double thickness of tinsel and results in a microscopically thicker body, but I do not consider this to be of any material consequence.

Run the silk down to the tail of the fly and back again to the front end, close-butting turns being essential to provide the smooth base for the tinsel. Now cut off about eight inches of the flat tinsel of appropriate width and tie in one end of this under the shank at the front end. Whip this down with a couple of turns of silk.

Next, wind the tinsel carefully down to the tail in butting but not overlapping turns and then back to the front end. Any excrescence left at the front end will be hidden by the subsequent winding of the hackle.

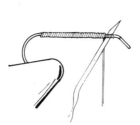

Tinsel tied in

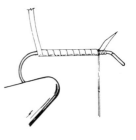

Tinsel wound to tail

Tinsel wound forward again ready for securing

This method obviates any offensive lump at the tail and any small gaps inadvertently left on the rearward winding will probably be covered up on the return journey.

On occasion this method may not be practicable and it will be necessary to tie the tinsel in at the tail and wind it forwards in a single layer

If you just tie the tinsel in under the shank as mentioned above and then wind it forwards you are very apt to produce that unsightly bulge that we are trying to avoid, and a better method which is more likely to give a neater start is that described by John Veniard in his excellent book *Fly-tying Problems and their Answers*:

Trim the end of the tinsel to a "chisel" point (a single oblique cut) and holding it tightly place this point under the shank at the tail end, pointing away from you and with the sloping edge at an angle of 90° to the shank: this means that the long end of the tinsel will slant slightly forwards. Secure the end with a turn of silk, then fold the point of the tinsel over anti-clockwise round the shank. A tight "figure-of-eight" turn of silk should then be taken over it to hold the point down in position.

Carry on with close-butting turns of silk back to the front end, then wind the tinsel carefully forward in even turns, not overlapping or leaving gaps. The slope from the "chisel" point should enable you to get away to a neat start.

Whichever of these methods is used you will need to secure the tinsel at the forward end and this is the best way of so doing:

When the front end is reached hold the tinsel taut with one hand while you take a tight turn of silk round it with the other. Bend the waste end of the tinsel back over that turn, as close as possible, and take two further turns rearwards over it. You can now either cut the waste tinsel away or "waggle" it backwards and forwards a few times so that it breaks off cleanly at the tie. Tinsel secured in this way is unlikely to come adrift.

If it is desired to produce a tinsel body somewhat more bulky, build up a smooth underbody first by winding on very tightly a length of floss-silk.

It can also prove worth while to smear the surface of any underbody (either tying-silk or floss) with a thin coat of clear adhesive before winding on the tinsel. This will help to prevent the whole thing unravelling if the tinsel breaks or gets cut by the teeth of a fish.

Polythene
Clear polythene wound over a smooth tinsel underbody gives a remarkable "transparent" effect and is very useful for such imitations of fish or fry as the "Polystickle".

The easiest way of using this material is to take a strip of fairly stout polythene about six inches long and about half an inch wide, stretch this thoroughly by pulling it (in short sections at a time) almost to its breaking-point and then trim it to a narrow strip about $\frac{1}{16}$-inch wide.

Tie this in and wind it over the body in one or two thicknesses as required.

As a possibly easier substitute for this, try a length of this horrible modern transparent plastic string. Unravel and flatten it thoroughly before using it in narrow strips.

COMMON BODY FAULTS

These will be perpetrated not only by the beginner but all too frequently by the more experienced dresser. Those most likely to be seen are:
(a) The body built up too close to the eye of the hook. (Watch out for this one all the time.)
(b) Uneven winding.
(c) Too much dubbing material applied.
(d) Overlapping or gaps in what should be a smooth body.

RIBBING
As already stated, the object of this is twofold; first to give a

segmented or transparent appearance to the fly and secondly to strengthen the body dressing against the sharp teeth of a predatory fish. It also adds a suggestion of "flash" to a fly.

Ribbing can be carried out with either flat, round or oval tinsel, with fine wire or with coloured floss or thread.

If the body is to be ribbed, it is usual to tie in the ribbing material at the tail end of the hook before tying-in and winding-on the body material and it should be held or clipped out of the way while the body is being dealt with. (This is where a clip on the barrel of the vice comes in useful. See Chapter 1.)

When using flat tinsel for ribbing trim the end to a "chisel" point and tie this in as for a tinsel body. If round or oval tinsel is used hold the end of the length of tinsel firmly and pull the last quarter of an inch smartly between the nails of the thumb and finger of the other hand; this will unravel the wire covering and expose the silk core. Cut away the wire and fray out the core, which can then be tied-in easily and securely.

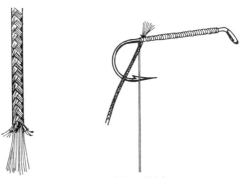

Round or oval tinsel for ribbing

Solid wire used for ribbing is usually of very fine gauge and being highly polished tends to pull out very easily. If you "nick" or kink the wire with the thumbnail about a sixteenth of an inch from the end this tendency to slip should be effectively eliminated.

When the body material has been wound on and is ready for the ribbing, take hold of the loose end of the ribbing material and, working in the reverse direction to the "lay" of the body material, take one complete turn round the shank of the hook immediately behind the tail end of the body, thus making a neat and definite finish to the tail end.

Keeping the hand holding the ribbing material close to the hook and continuing to hold it taut wind it in an evenly spaced spiral of turns about ⅛-inch apart up the body to the front end, where it should be secured in the appropriate manner with the tying-silk. Secure flat tinsel as you did when winding a tinsel body and if using round or oval tinsel hold the end taut as you trap it with a turn of silk, then cut off the waste leaving a tag about quarter of an inch long projecting. Fray this out as you did when tying it in originally and secure it with a couple more turns of the silk. If there is sufficient material left to make it worth while put these waste ends in the "snippets" box for use on another occasion.

The point of winding the ribbing material in the opposite direction to that in which the body is wound is again twofold. Not only does it secure the turns of body material more firmly but if the lay of the ribbing follows that of the body material the ribbing may bite or bed down between the turns of body material and become virtually hidden.

COMMON RIBBING FAULTS

Again these apply not only to the novice. The more usual faults are:
(a) Irregular or unevenly spaced turns. These ruin the look of a fly.
(b) Ribbing turns too close together. Sometimes a fly appears to have more ribbing than body, so check this tendency to "overdo" ribbing.
(c) Ribbing not securely fastened at the front end.

TAIL ENDS
The after end of a fly is often adorned with a tail; sometimes this is

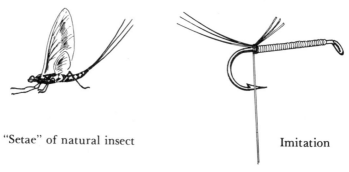

"Setae" of natural insect   Imitation

merely a traditional decoration but in the case of certain flies, both dry and wet, it may be a deliberate imitation of the tail or "whisks" of the insect. These appendages are known to the entomologist as the "setae".

The tail is usually the first component to be tied-in after running-on the first layer of tying-silk.

Taking as an example the deliberate imitation, the setae of a small insect can be represented by two or more (according to the particular insect being copied) single fibres from a large cock hackle of appropriate colour.

To tie-in the tail first make sure that there is an even "bed" of tying-silk on which it can rest; remember that you cannot tie any natural material satisfactorily direct on to a bare shank. Then take the required number of fibres and either cut or flick them off the quill. If it is desired to have one fibre of the tail longer than the others now is the time to adjust it.

Leaving the tying-silk hanging under tension at the rear end of the body, with the forefinger and thumb of the right hand place the bunch of fibres in their required position at the end of the body on top of the shank and then extend the grip of the thumb and finger to embrace the shank itself. If this is done there is no danger of the bunch of fibres changing position while the next step is carried out.

Now grip first the shank and then the bunch of fibres with the thumb and forefinger of the left hand (thumb on the "home" side of the hook) and release the right hand. The bunch of fibres should now be in position ready for tying-in, held there by the left hand.

Devote some time to practising this "positioning" and adjustment (see Chapter 5).

Keeping the tying-silk taut, bring it up with the right hand in a clockwise direction and guide it between the tips of the left thumb and finger on the "home" side of the bunch of fibres, that is to say between the bunch of fibres and the inside of the thumb.

Nipping the silk there with the left hand, bring the silk over and down again vertically on the "away" side (between the bunch and the ball of the finger) and over the far side of the shank. Maintaining a firm but not too tight hold of the bunch of fibres with the left hand, draw the silk down steadily vertically so that it binds the fibres down on top of the shank without spreading out or rolling round.

Repeat this performance with a couple more turns of silk, then release the left hand and check that the bunch of fibres has been tied securely in its proper position. If it has not, unwind the silk and tie it again; it is usually a waste of time to try to pull it into position.

You can have the tail drooping or sticking out horizontally to the rear if you so wish but if you prefer it to "cock" up a little, lift the tail upwards and forwards and take another turn of silk immediately behind it; this is what is meant by giving it a "kick". Trim off the waste butts of fibre.

Other tails for flies may consist of a tuft of wool or floss-silk (teased out with a needle after being tied-in), a slip of web from a wing feather or a bunch of hair fibres. These are all tied-in by the same basic method, but if slips of wing feather are used it is best to take a pair of slips from matching opposite (right and left) feathers. These are handled in much the same way as the wings of a wet fly (q.v.).

The length of the tail is largely a matter of personal preference and "beauty being in the eye of the beholder". If it looks to be in reasonable proportion it is probably right.

Some flies are like a Manx Cat in that they have no tail.

TAGS

Sometimes, usually for traditional salmon and sea-trout dressings, a "tag" is tied before the tail is applied. This often consists of two or three close-butted turns of round or oval tinsel which is tied-in like the ribbing tinsel and then wound on and secured with a couple of turns of tying-silk, the tail then being tied-in between the tag and the rear end of the body.

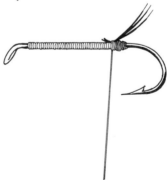

If the body is to be ribbed later with the same type of tinsel leave the waste end of the tag for this purpose, otherwise it should be trimmed away.

Occasionally a second tag (sometimes referred to as a "tip") of coloured floss or fluorescent material is tied-in between the tinsel tag and the tail and this second winding of floss will neatly cover up the turns of tying-silk securing the first tag.

BUTTS
The more ornate fly may sometimes call for a "butt" in its dressing. This usually consists of two or three close turns of teased-out wool or some fibrous herl such as Peacock or Ostrich and again will neatly cover any joints.

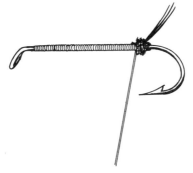

COMMON FAULTS ON TAIL-ENDS
(a) Tail too long or too short. The fly should not look out of balance. This is usually due to movement of the bunch of fibres between its being originally positioned and actually tied-in.

(b) Tail twisted to one side, caused by not holding firm enough and allowing it to slip round as it is being tied-in. There is less likelihood of this happening if the tail is tied down on a proper "bed" of smooth turns of tying-silk and the dresser works with his hands close to the hook.

(c) Untidy or "gappy" tags or butts.

7

HACKLES

Having completed the body and tail we now turn our attention to the front end of the fly where we attach the hackle, the basic idea of which is to represent the legs of a struggling insect.

Always remember to match the size of the hackle to the size of the hook used; as a rough guide the length of the hackle fibres should be approximately equal to the distance between the eye of the hook and its point.

COLLAR HACKLES

The simplest form of hackle for a dry fly or for a wingless wet fly is the "collar" hackle, so called because the fibres of the hackle feather radiate in a collar or ruff round the neck of the hook used.

For a dry or floating fly we want a hackle with stiff springy fibres that will float lightly on the surface of the water so a good quality hackle from the neck of a mature cockerel is selected (see Chapter 4, page 35).

Choose a hackle of the appropriate length of fibres and strip away the useless flue from its base until good "clean" individual fibres are reached; do this stripping in small doses (say a quarter of an inch) at a time rather than try to rip the whole lot off at once, which will damage the hackle.

Hold the hackle by its tip and draw it several times through the fingers of the other hand in order to separate the web fibres and make them stand away from the quill.

With the left hand hold the hackle near the bottom of the remaining web and place the stem under the shank of the hook immediately to the right of the tying-silk which is hanging down (weighted) ready. The stem should point away from you, slightly to your right and slightly upwards, the fibres perpendicular to the hook shank and the "bright" or outer side of the hackle facing the eye of the hook.

Holding the hackle firmly in this position with the left hand bring up the tying-silk in a clockwise turn with your right, keeping it very taut and keeping the hand close to the hook, to trap the stem or quill.

A common but undesirable happening at this stage is that the
hackle stem twists, altering the angle of the fibres in relation to the
shank and in extreme cases bringing the "dull" or inner side of the
hackle to the front. The tendency for this to happen will be
considerably reduced if the hackle is held firmly in position as it is
tied-in. If this does occur, unwind the silk and start again.

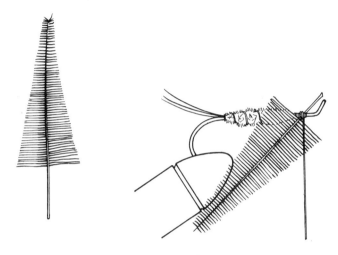

Tying in a hackle by its stem

Bring the next turn of silk to the left of the hackle stem below the
shank and pass it over the shank to the right of the "waste" stem
thus forming a "figure-of-eight" tying which makes for a secure
hold. Give the hackle a pull to check that it is firmly held.

Leaving the silk hanging again under tension take hold of the
stem of the hackle towards the tip, either with the fingers or with
the hackle-pliers. Be careful to clip the pliers on to the actual stem
and not merely on the web fibres, which are delicate and easily
broken or cut.

Keeping the hand close to the hook, which will help you to avoid
allowing the hackle to twist, wind the hackle forward in close turns
round the neck of the fly so that the web fibres stick out all round in
a neat collar of the required size. Four such turns are usually
enough for the average dry fly.

Holding the end of the hackle very taut with one hand, with the

TYPES OF HACKLE

Wet Fly	Dry Fly	"Palmer"
	Winged Wet Fly	"False"

other wind the tying-silk (also very taut) two or three times through the hackle collar thus formed, finishing in front of the turns of hackle. If you "swing" the taut silk from side to side as you make these turns the silk will pass down between the individual fibres and bite down on the coils of quill or stem.

Wet the fingers and press all the hackle fibres towards the rear of the hook and take a final turn of silk in front of them to secure the hackle.

With the fine-pointed scissors snip off close to the shank the "stub" of the hackle and the waste end of its tip, being careful not to cut the tying-silk in the process. (Do not throw away any undamaged hackle-tips; put them in the "snippets" box for later use as hackle-tip wings. See Chapter 8, page 104.)

An alternative method is to tie-in the hackle by its tip and wind it holding the butt end of the feather. Again draw the hackle through the fingers leaving the tip "separated" for tying-in. This is a good way of using up hackle feathers the lower fibres of which are too long for a small fly.

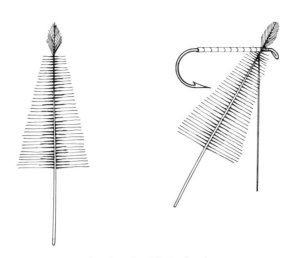

Tying in a hackle by its tip

Whichever method is used, pick out with the point of the dubbing-needle any hackle fibres which may have got caught up in the tying and are pointing in the wrong direction.

The same procedure applies for tying the hackle of a wingless or "hackled" wet fly but in this latter case a less generous dressing is called for, two or three turns of hackle being ample. As a fly of this type requires a hackle with softer fibres which will move freely in the water a hackle from the neck of a domestic hen is commonly used for this purpose.

* * *

Many "bought" flies are over-hackled.

HACKLES FOR WINGED WET FLIES
Where a winged wet fly is being made the hackle is first tied in the same way as before, but we have to go a stage further.

When the collar hackle has been tied and trimmed, with the dubbing-needle divide equally that portion of the hackle that protrudes from the top of the shank. Wet the tips of the thumb and finger and pull *all* the hackle fibres below the shank, at the same time slanting them to the rear.

To hold them in this position take three or four close-butting turns of silk towards the rear. This not only secures the hackle in the shape required but also provides the necessary bed of silk on which

AT LEFT	MIDDLE	AT RIGHT
Cock hackle	Hen hackle	Partridge hackle
Prepared for use	Prepared for use	Prepared for use
Tied in by stem	Tied in by stem	Tied in by stem
Tied in by tip	Tied in by tip	

to tie the wing at a later stage. (See Chapter 8.)

Once again, if you have estimated the size of the hackle correctly the ends of the hackle fibres should just reach the point of the hook without masking it unduly.

TYING A HACKLE FOR A WET FLY

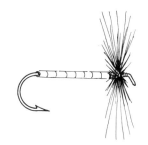

Hackle tied and secured

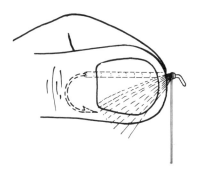

All fibres brought below shank

Fibres secured below shank

"PALMER" HACKLES

On occasion, instead of tying the hackle as a neat collar at the head of the fly it is desired to spread it over the length of the body to give the effect of a hairy caterpillar. (In mediaeval times a pilgrim or wanderer was known as a "palmer" and this term is applied to caterpillars of the "Woolly Bear" type by reason of their habit of wandering.)

To tie a palmer hackle prepare the hackle feather as before and either tie-in the hackle by the stem at the head of the fly and wind it in a neat spiral down to the tail end of the body, where it can be secured by the ribbing material, trimming off the waste tip, or alternatively tie it in by the tip at the tail end before you wind on the body material, which will of course cover the tied-in tip. Spiral it neatly up the body to the front end and secure it there with the tying-silk.

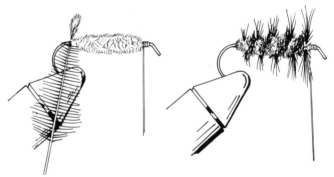

Palmer hackle tied in by its tip at rear of body

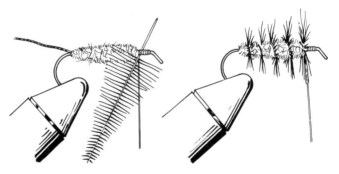

Palmer hackle tied in by stem at head and secured by ribbing material

Whichever method is used pick out any caught-up fibres with the dubbing-needle.

Never tie the hackle in by its stem at the tail or by its tip at the head or you will get the taper effect of the palmer hackle reversed.

"DOUBLING" A HACKLE

Some traditional salmon-fly dressings call for a "body" hackle which is wound in a manner somewhat similar to our "palmer".

Whereas the palmer should have as bushy or "buzz" appearance as possible in order to imitate the hairy caterpillar, the salmon-fly body-hackle should be more streamlined with all the fibres sloping to the rear. For this purpose a really professional neat body-hackle will be produced if the hackle is doubled before it is spiralled on, i.e. the hackle is folded so that all the fibres lie on the same side of the quill and are not crushed or caught-up as the hackle is wound on.

To achieve this, tie-in the tip of the hackle firmly at the tail end of the body. Holding the stem very taut with one hand, wet the fingers of the other and "fold" all the fibres to the rear, "bright" or outer side outwards. The wetter you can make the fibres the better they will go where you want them and it is advisable to wind on the doubled hackle as quickly as possible before it dries and the fibres resume their normal position. Wound on carefully without twisting or catching up fibres, this will give a neat tapered effect instead of something resembling a tangled brush.

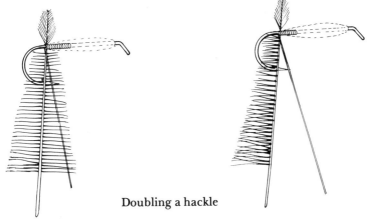

Doubling a hackle

An alternative method of producing a hackle with the fibres on one side only of the stem is to strip all the fibres off one side. It must be remembered that the result is only half the thickness of the "doubled" hackle and this will show in the appearance of the finished fly.

"FALSE", "BEARD" or "CHIN" HACKLES
Although this is technically "cheating" in that the quill of the hackle is not used, this method of tying a hackle for a wet fly has

TYING A FALSE HACKLE

Hook reversed in vice

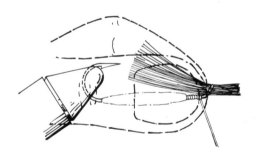

Hackle fibres positioned for tying

Tied and trimmed

certain points to recommend it:

(a) You can use up hackles whose fibres are far too long for the size of hook used.
(b) It is a quicker method.
(c) It avoids a hump where the hackle is tied-in and makes for a smoother and more sleek finish.

To tie a false hackle, pull off a bunch of fibres from one side of the quill of a hackle feather; be careful to get the points of the fibres level. Hold this bunch of fibres in position at the throat of the fly and tie it in as you did the tail (see Chapter 6).

You will probably find this easier if you remove the hook from the vice, turn it through 180° (so that you are winding up the silk and not unwinding it) and replace it in the vice upside-down before tying in the bunch of fibres.

When the false hackle has been tied securely trim off carefully any stubs of fibre projecting in front of the tie. This cut should slope towards the eye.

A tuft of hair fibres can be used instead of feather, but in this case the use of a small drop of varnish on the "bed" is recommended (see Hair wings, Chapter 8).

"PARACHUTE" or HORIZONTAL HACKLES

Here the hackle is in the same horizontal plane as the shank of the hook instead of being perpendicular to it. This feature makes for light landing and good flotation.

So far as I can ascertain, this type of fly was invented by a Canadian angler some forty or so years ago and was taken up and patented under the name "Parachute" by the firm of Alex Martin of Glasgow. It is still produced and marketed under that name by their successors, John Dickson & Co.

Hackles of this type are quite easy to tie and there are several methods of doing it:

Method 1

Having checked that there is a smooth "bed", strip the flue and excess fibre from a hackle of suitable size, leaving a clean "stalk". Place the hackle thus prepared along the top of the shank with the stripped butt facing straight forwards, "bright" or convex side downwards and whip this down with three or four secure turns of silk.

Bend the waste stem upwards and take another firm turn of silk immediately in front of it. Double the stem over so as to make an upright loop about a quarter of an inch high and secure this with another turn of silk. Trim off the waste end.

Hook reversed in vice,
stripped hackle tied in

Loop formed and secured

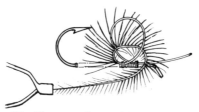

Hackle wound round base of loop

Stem and loop trimmed off

With the fingers or the hackle-pliers take hold of the hackle and wind it three or four horizontal turns round the base of the loop. Secure it in this position by passing the tying-silk through the hackle fibres and trim off the waste tip of the hackle.

Trim the outstanding loop of quill as close as possible to the shank and place a small drop of varnish or adhesive in the centre of the hackle to prevent it slipping off.

Special hooks incorporating a short stem perpendicular to the shank can be bought, but these are not really worth the extra expense.

Method 2
A more secure and efficient way of tying this type of hackle is to use Messrs. Veniards' "Bob Barlow" Parachute Attachment. This consists of a "gallows" fitted above the vice which carries a spring-loaded hook to hold up the loop during the winding of the hackle. (If however you can get an assistant to take the place of this device you can dispense with it!)

Tie the hackle in, form the loop and secure it as you did in Method 1.

Clip the hook of the attachment into the loop.

Hackle stem looped and secured

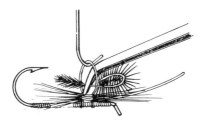

Hackle wound, tip being drawn
back through loop

Wind the hackle three or four times round the base of the loop and then pass the tip of the hackle through the loop. Take hold of this tip (it is easier to do this using hackle-pliers or dental forceps) and work all the spare hackle through. Disengage the attachment or tell your assistant that his services are no longer required.

Holding the webbed end of the hackle firmly, with the other hand draw the end of the stem steadily forward until it closes the loop and secures the hackle. Trim off the waste ends of hackle tip and stem and make the hackle doubly secure with a couple of turns of silk as before.

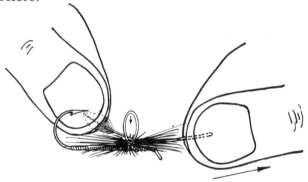

Stem drawn to close loop

Method 3. The "Murdoch" Method

This way of tying this type of hackle was devised by the late Mr. Jack Murdoch, a Scots veterinary surgeon practising in Essex, and like most simple ways of doing things is extremely efficient.

For this the only extra equipment needed is a knitting-needle of a diameter of just under a quarter of an inch, say a size 6.

Knitting needle inserted into loop

Make the loop of hackle stem above the shank as you did for the other methods.

From the far side of the hook insert about an inch of the knitting-needle into the loop, which it should fit closely. Rest the other end of the needle on a box or something convenient so that it is roughly level.

Take hold of the tip of the hackle with the heavier pair of hackle-pliers and take three or four turns of the hackle horizontally between the upper surface of the hook shank and the underside of the needle. This will ensure that the hackle is wound close against the body.

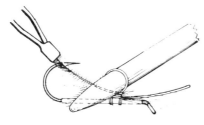

Hackle wound between needle and shank

Leaving the hackle tip hanging down on your side of the hook kept taut by the weight of the hackle-pliers, gently rotate the needle to loosen it very slightly and then withdraw it, again from the far side.

Still working from the far side insert the nose of another pair of hackle-pliers (or preferably fine-pointed dental forceps if you have a pair) through the loop and take hold of the dangling tip. When this is firmly held you can release the original hackle-pliers used to wind the hackle.

Needle withdrawn, tip being drawn back through loop

Draw the tip back through the loop from the far side, freeing any caught-up fibres with the dubbing-needle, and tighten and finish as in Method 2.

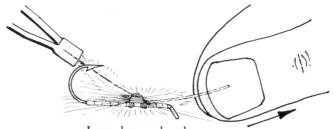

Loop drawn closed

Instead of the knitting-needle you can use the butt of a quill about $\frac{1}{4}$-inch thick and about an inch long, which will "sit" happily on top of the shank without support. Scrape the end of the quill smooth and polish it so that it does not stick when rotated in the loop.

Whichever of these methods is used, if you wish to form the hackle underneath the shank so as to lift the fly on the water as much as possible, remove the hook from the vice and replace it upside-down (as for a false hackle, q.v.) so that the hackle finishes up below the shank.

If on the other hand you think that the colour or silhouette of the body as seen by the fish should be exposed, tie the hackle above the shank. This is a matter of personal preference.

CLIPPING HACKLES

Before leaving this subject of hackles, a word on the practice of "clipping" hackles may not be out of place. Sometimes a novice (and even an old hand can be guilty of it) will find that the finished hackle is too long and will attempt to rectify matters by trimming it down with a pair of scissors. While this does not matter so much in the case of a dry fly (indeed there are tools on the market for trimming oversize hackles before use), a wet fly treated in this way looks far too hard and unnatural. The answer is of course to measure and position the hackle properly before tying it in.

COMMON FAULTS IN HACKLES

(a) Tying the hackle too close to the front end of the hook, thus "crowding" the eye.

(b) Using a hackle of the wrong size for the fly.

(c) Allowing the hackle to twist during tying.

(d) Uneven or excessive "palmering".

(e) The hackle of a wet fly lying too close to the shank owing to the securing turns of silk being carried too far back.

8

WINGS

Before starting to tie-in any sort of wing it must be remembered that you cannot tie any form of wing direct on to the bare metal of a hook; if you attempt to do so it will invariably slip round the shank. We therefore first check that the place where the wing is to be tied-in is covered with several close-butted turns of silk to make a smooth "bed".

PREPARING WING-SLIPS

Paired Secondaries
Matched slips
from opposite feathers

Segments marked off
Ready
for tying

Although feather fibre has been the traditional material for wings for literally hundreds of years and the use of animal hair for this purpose is of more recent origin, hair wings are the easiest to deal with so we will start with them.

TYPES OF WING

Hairwing	Wet Fly	Sedge
Upwinged dry fly	"Spent" pattern	Mayfly
	Streamer	

HAIR WINGS

Having run-on the "bed" of close-butted turns of silk, apply a drop of clear varnish to this bed, on top of the shank.

From a piece of hide with the hair still on it separate off a bunch or tuft of hairs of the estimated size required and, holding the tips of the hairs level snip off this tuft close to the skin. Holding the tuft firmly brush out its base thoroughly to get rid of any fluffy "undercoat" leaving the long "guard" hairs for our wing; an old stiff toothbrush is ideal for this.

Here again, positioning is all-important so hold the tuft of hair between the right thumb and finger and place it in position on the bed so that the tips of the hair project beyond the bend of the hook for the required distance (usually about half as much as the overall length of the hook).

If you then extend the grip of that thumb and finger to embrace the hook shank the wing tuft will not move its position when you carry out the next step, which is to change the hands over. Retaining the hold with the right hand, grip first the shank and then the tuft of hair with the thumb and forefinger of the left. Then release the right hand.

Holding the wing tuft firmly in position thus bring the tying-silk up (taut) between the tips of the left thumb and finger, the silk passing on the "home" side, i.e. between the ball of the thumb and the wing. Bring the silk down again between the tips of the finger and thumb, this time on the "away" side, i.e. between the wing and the inside of the finger. Draw the silk down vertically and you will feel the tuft of hair being tightened down on to the bed. Repeat this with two or three more turns of silk then release the hold of the left hand and check that the wing has been tied down in its proper position.

Hair fibres positioned and tied in

As the hairs are separate fibres not fastened to each other in any way like the web of a feather they must be secured against pulling out. While the drop of varnish that was applied to the bed will help in this, they should be further secured by lifting the wing tuft upwards and forwards and taking a complete (360°) turn of tying-silk in a clockwise direction horizontally round the base of the wing where it springs from the hook. Lower the wing again and take two or three more turns of silk rearwards to cover up this "locking" turn.

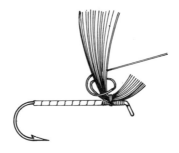

Horizontal turn of silk round wing-root

"Locking" turn

Finally, lift up the stub of waste hair from in front of the tie and holding it as near vertical as possible snip off the stub close to the tie. This should result in a trim sloping down to the eye and the job is completed by covering this slope with neat turns of silk to form the head.

HAIR-WINGED DRY FLIES

Small tufts of thin hair can be used for the wings of dry flies. When the wing has been tied-in (in much the same manner as above), split the wing tuft into two equal portions with "figure-of-eight" turns of silk and get the resulting wing as upright as possible.

FEATHER WING WET FLIES

First, remember the necessity for the "bed" of tying-silk.

It is advisable to practise first with feathers with a fairly "strong" fibre such as those from a domestic fowl or Pheasant.

Match up a pair of secondary feathers, i.e. corresponding feathers from the right and left wings of the same bird. The camber of the web should show a shallow even curve.

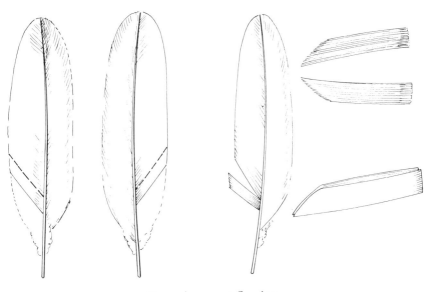

Preparing a wet-fly wing

Strip away all the fluffy "flue" from the base of the feather until firm clean fibre is reached, then measure off a segment of web of the required width, say about $\frac{3}{16}$-inch for a size 10 hook. Part the web at this point with the dubbing-needle (inserting the point of the needle at the quill and working outwards) and cut the segment out at its base. Cut towards the base of the stem otherwise you may damage the remaining web and waste it. Some dressers prefer to strip these segments from the quill with the fingers; they find that a shaving of quill comes away with the segment and holds the web fibres together.

Having checked that the two segments are of exactly the same width, place one segment "bright" or outer side downwards on the bench and cover it exactly with its pair, the other segment being of course bright side uppermost. The "dull" or concave surfaces are thus face to face.

Pick up the pair of segments very carefully with the tweezers and make any adjustment that may be required such as the removal of excess fibre from one side, then take hold of them with the right forefinger and thumb so that the "leading" or convex edge is uppermost. Keeping the section vertical, place the lower concave or "trailing" edge of the wing segment on top of the shank and move it until the point of the wing just protrudes beyond the bend of the hook.

When you are satisfied with its position extend the grip of the right thumb and finger to embrace the shank of the hook and then change over to the left hand as you did when positioning the hair wing.

With the right hand bring up the taut silk between the thumb and finger of the left hand, and between the thumb and the wing segment (the "home" side), and then down on the "away" side, i.e. between the wing and the finger. Draw the silk down steadily, keeping it vertical, and hold the segment firmly with the left hand as you do this so that the segment folds down on the bed like a "concertina". Unless it is firmly held during this stage the wing will always fold over to one side and produce a "corkscrew" effect.

Take two more turns of tying-silk maintaining this hold then release the left hand and check that the wing is sitting in its correct position. If it is not satisfactory, unwind the tying turns and start again with a fresh pair of segments. If it is correct lift the stub in front of the tie and trim it off as neatly as possible.

Again, practise first with a fairly big hook (say a size 6 or 8, old scale) and then graduate to the smaller sizes.

When proficiency has been attained using this type of feather the beginner can proceed to tackle more difficult wing feathers. These include smaller and more delicate feathers such as those of the

Starling and also the "softer" types like the blue wing feathers from a Mallard drake or the black and white speckled shoulder feathers from a Teal drake. In these cases the fibres tend to part company and spread like a fan. If the fibres do fan out in this way after being tied-in, a quick lick or a stroke with wet fingers will soon bring them together again. All such feathers are tied-in by the same basic method, the only difference being the extra care which has to be taken in handling them.

Sometimes instead of a wing feather one uses a tail feather in order to make the wing of a fly. While the shorter type of tail feather (e.g. Rook, Magpie, etc.) is very similar in form to a wing secondary, in the case of a long tail such as that of a hen Pheasant the angle of the web fibres relative to the quill is very much more acute and the fibres will need some adjustment and reshaping before being used.

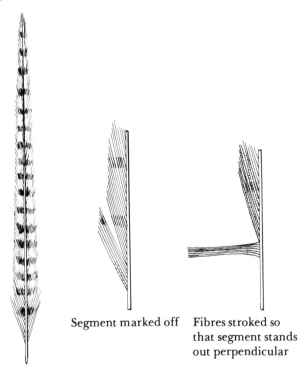

Segment marked off   Fibres stroked so
that segment stands
out perpendicular

Using a hen pheasant centre tail for wing

Mark off equal matching segments as you did for the wing secondaries, then with the fingers stroke these out so that they stand out as near perpendicular to the quill as you can get them. Owing to the little "zip-fastener" hooks or barbules on the web fibres these will re-engage to form a segment similar to that from a wing feather.

"MARRIED" WINGS

This capability for web fibres to link up with each other can be put to another use, to produce a wing made up of different colours or even varieties of feather joined or "married" into one composite segment. While this process is mainly used for the old traditional salmon-fly dressings it is also applied in certain trout patterns (e.g. "Parmachene Belle").

To make a married wing, select matched pairs (right and left) of the feathers you propose to join. Let us take as an example a pair of white feathers and a pair of red, from which we will make a wing white at the bottom and red on top.

Take the white feather which has the bright or outer surface of the web on the left hand side of the quill and cut out a narrow segment (three or four fibres only). Do the same with the "left-handed" red feather.

Hold the slip of white feather between the thumb and finger of the left hand, "dull" side towards you, *convex* edge upwards and the point to your left. Now place the bottom or *concave* edge of the red feather (also dull side towards you) along the top edge of the white and carefully take hold of the bases of both segments with the right hand. Stroke the two segments together gently with the left hand until they make a smooth join. Place the composite segment thus made "bright" side downwards on the bench.

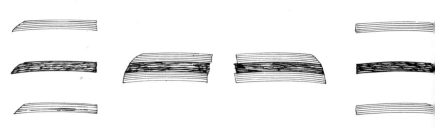

Building up a "married" wing segment

Repeat this performance with the "right-handed" feathers, in which case the "bright" side will be towards you if the points face to the left.

Place the second composite segment exactly over the first, "dull" sides inwards, and tie the composite wing in as for any ordinary wet fly wing.

While this "marrying" process is comparatively easy where segments of feather from the same type of bird are used (for example, Swan dyed red and Goose left white), extra care is called for when dealing with dissimilar types. A case in point is the tail feather of Golden Pheasant, sometimes married to other feathers to make the wing of the traditional salmon-fly, which seems to have a particular aversion to joining with other fibres.

"ROLLED" WINGS

As an alternative method of tying a wing which needs to lie closer to the shank, such as is required for a "Sedge" pattern, the rolled wing is both effective and easy to tie. Perhaps "folded" is a better description than "rolled".

For this you need only use one wing feather, preferably with good adhesion between the individual web fibres. Feathers such as Teal shoulder, the fibres of which tend to spring apart, may not be so easy to handle in this way.

First mark off a segment of web about three times as wide as the wing you wish to tie and stroke this out with the fingers so that the segment stands out as near perpendicular to the quill as possible, with the tips of the fibres level, and cut this segment away at its base.

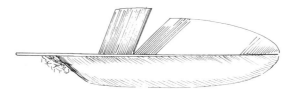

Place the segment bright side downwards on a level surface and with a needle or tweezers turn up one third and fold it down over the remainder.

Now fold the third from the opposite edge over the double thickness thus formed and you should have a wing segment three times as thick as the original web and one-third of its original width, showing the bright side on both exposed surfaces.

Flat wing segment   Folded   Ready for tying

Place this in position on the "bed" with the "open" edge downwards and tie it in as for an ordinary wet fly wing, remembering that a "Sedge" wing should project beyond the bend of the hook slightly more than the usual type.

"UP-WINGED" DRY FLY WINGS

This to my mind is one of the most difficult processes in fly-dressing and when you can tie a neat up-winged dry fly on a size 16 hook you are entitled to put up your fly-tyer's badge!

Once again I would advise the beginner to give himself some considerable practice in this, starting on a fairly big hook (say a size 8 or 10, old scale) with segments of a "strong" fibred feather. Only when fully conversant with this should he progress to smaller hooks and the more delicate wing feathers such as those of the Starling.

The first stage is simple; having run-on the bed of tying-silk as usual cut two corresponding segments from a matched pair of wing feathers as you did for the wet fly.

Place one segment exactly over the other, but this time it is the reverse of what you did for the wet fly. The bright or outer surfaces of the segments should face inwards so that the segments tend to stand apart when held by the base.

Again in reverse of the wet fly procedure, the concave or trailing edge of the wing segment is uppermost so that the points of the wing curve upwards and forwards.

Tie in the wing with three turns of silk just as you did with the wet fly wing, being very careful again to get the same neat "concertina" fold. It will assist you in the next stage if you now secure the work with a half-hitch.

Wing slips
curving outwards

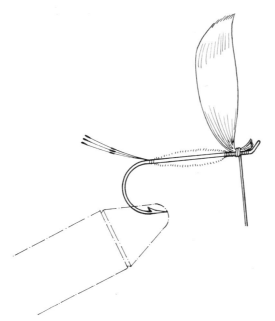

Wing segment curving upwards and forwards

Now comes the really tricky part of the job; lift the wing forward and take a complete 360° horizontal turn (clockwise) round the root of the wing immediately above the shank, dropping the silk down on the far side of the shank. (A half turn is not sufficient.) This process is made easier if you use the tip of a finger to hold the wing root steady as you take the horizontal turn of silk with the other hand.

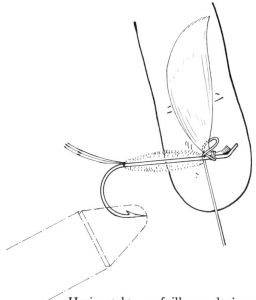

Horizontal turn of silk round wing-root

The next step is possibly even more demanding; part the wings very carefully with the dubbing-needle and open them out slightly, being particularly careful to avoid splitting the individual fibres of either wing segment. (Some people treat the wing segments first by painting them over with solvent or very thin clear varnish to avoid this splitting, but to my mind this spoils the appearance of the finished fly.) Again it may help if you place the tip of a finger of the left hand against the wing root as you carry out this part of the operation.

Now bring the silk up and pass it between the wings, in front of the right hand wing and behind the left. Bring it round again, this time behind the right and in front of the left. You have thus "spread" the wings with a figure-of-eight of silk.

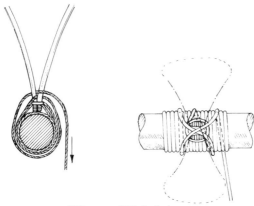

"Figure of Eight" tie

Be careful not to apply too much tension to the silk as you do this or the wings will be splayed out too much.

Finally, take one further tight turn of the silk immediately behind the wing root (ready to tie in the hackle). Trim the stubs neat and close.

DOUBLE SPLIT WINGS
An upwinged or split-wing dry fly made with doubled wing segments not only looks more attractive but also seems to "sit" better on the water. Once the knack of tying a single split-wing has been acquired this further development can be attempted.

Take two exactly equal segments from the same feather and place one over the other to form a double thickness. Do the same with segments from the opposite feather and place the two pairs together convex surfaces inwards as was done with the singles.

The double-thickness wing so formed is then tied-in and dealt with as before.

"SPENT" WINGS
The perfect insect after its final body-moult or ecdysis is known as the Imago or Spinner and after mating (and egg-laying in the case of the female) it falls exhausted on the water as a "Spent Spinner", an easy prey to the fish.

The wings of the spent spinner are best formed by using the extreme tips of cock hackles. Select a matched pair of cock hackles of the appropriate colour and size and strip from the quills all the web fibres except for those at the extreme tips; leave about $\frac{3}{8}$-inch in the case of the usual small dry fly pattern. You may find these prepared tips easier to handle if you shorten the stripped quill to about an inch from the start of the tip thus left.

Having wound on the usual bed of silk, place one of these tips on top of the shank, dull side uppermost and pointing horizontally to the left of the shank, i.e. away from you. Tie it in this position with a couple of turns of silk (in figure-of-eight).

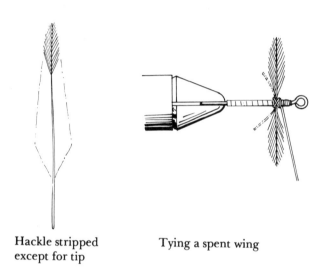

Hackle stripped   Tying a spent wing
except for tip

Repeat this with the other tip pointing towards you.

When you are satisfied that you have a pair of wings projecting equally either side from the shank and horizontal when looked at from the front, secure both in position with a further figure-of-eight turn and trim off the stubs as close to the tie as possible. The wings should not show what is known in aircraft recognition terminology as dihedral or anhedral, i.e. inclined above or below the horizontal plane.

An alternative and possibly easier method of tying a spent wing is to prepare the two hackle tips as before, place them together on the bed bright sides outwards and stems forward and tie them in as you would in the first stage of any winged fly. The tips can then be separated with the point of the dubbing-needle and the tying-silk passed between them in figure-of-eight turns to splay them out sideways, applying rather more tension on the silk in order to bring the wings down horizontal. Using this method it is easier to get the wings of equal length without having to adjust them.

"STREAMER" WINGS

A "streamer" fly or lure is presumably intended to represent some sort of small bait fish and is usually tied on a long-shanked hook with a long wing lying low along the shank. These are frequently tied as hairwings but if feathers are used they can be equally effective.

Although this again may be pure theory or prejudice, I think that many streamers are tied with too long a wing. If the end of the wing protrudes too far beyond the bend of the hook there is a possibility of a fish snapping at the harmless end of the wing instead of taking the "business" part of the hook.

Wings made from hair or from slips from a wing feather with a wide web are tied as already indicated, but very effective lures can be produced using long narrow cock hackles.

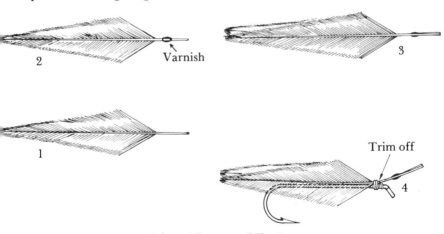

Tying a "Streamer Wing"

For these, take a matched pair of hackles and strip away all the flue and fibre from their bases leaving a tip of the length you require.

If it is proposed to fish the lure fast, place one prepared hackle over the other dull side to dull side, i.e. tending to curve inwards so that the lure moves easily through the water. If on the other hand you want a slow-fishing lure place them bright side to bright side so that they tend to curve apart and work with more of a fluttering movement.

Having wound on the usual bed, pick up a pair of prepared hackles and holding them very tightly place them in position on top of the shank and tie them in. If you fail to hold them very securely during the tying, the stem of one hackle may ride over the other and give a twisted wing. If this happens unwind it and start again.

You can "cheat" here by smearing the stripped stems with a tiny drop of adhesive or varnish, which will stick them together. This will not be noticed on the finished article as the "stuck" stems will have been trimmed off as waste.

Another nice streamer wing can be made by tying in a bunch of half a dozen strands of marabou, the fluffy feathers from the inside of the thigh of a white Turkey (either dyed or left natural white). These fibres move very freely in water.

"MATUKA" WINGS

A development of the streamer wing which is proving popular among reservoir fishermen is the "Matuka". This type of lure comes to us from New Zealand, the original patterns using feathers from a local bird of that name.

To tie this type of wing take a matched pair of fairly long hackles (cock or hen as called for by the recipe for the dressing) and strip away all the flue and fibres from their bases until the length of the remaining web is about twice the overall length of the hook.

Tie the body, leaving the ribbing wire or tinsel loose at the rear end and the tying-silk hanging at the front end. Make sure again of a good level "bed".

Place the hackle feathers exactly together, dull sides inwards, and then strip off the web fibres on one side of the stems for exactly the length of the body.

Hen hackles prepared

Tie the pair of hackles in firmly at the head end. Lower the stripped stems along the top surface of the body and then with the dubbing-needle part the vertical web fibres immediately above the rear end of the body.

Holding the wing firmly in position thus, with the other hand bring the ribbing material through that gap in the fibres so as to bind the stems down at the rear end of the body. Continue ribbing in the ordinary way, parting the web fibres again at each turn. This will result in a series of equal tufts of hackle fibre protruding vertically from the body.

Secure the ribbing material very firmly at the head end.

Wing completed

"FAN" WINGS

These are used when tying an imitation of the imago Mayfly and are usually made from the breast feathers of a duck, either left natural or dyed as required. These have a steep natural curve which renders them ideal for this purpose.

Take an evenly matched pair of feathers and strip away the flue and fibre until a triangular tip of about half to three quarters of an inch long is left.

After winding the usual bed place the wings together bright sides inwards so that they fan out when held at the base.

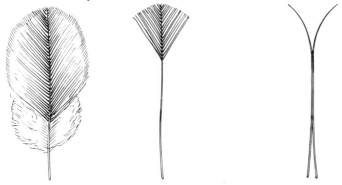

Duck Breast Feather   Stripped   Webs curving outwards
Preparing a Mayfly "Fan" wing

Holding the wings together firmly with the left hand place them on the bed with the stems pointing forwards and tie them in. Push the stems down either side of the shank, pointing forwards and downwards. Lift the wings forward and take two full turns of silk horizontally round the base of the wing.

Fold back the protruding stems parallel with the shank and tie them down with two or three turns of silk just behind the wing-root; trim off the waste ends. The wings should now sit up nicely on top of the shank.

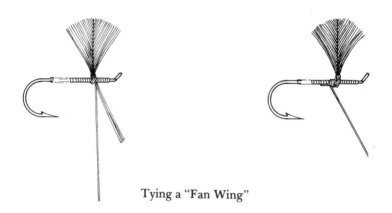

Tying a "Fan Wing"

AMERICAN DRY FLY WINGS

In the United States the usual dry fly wing is not tied in the English up-winged fashion but in a manner much more like the preceding "fan" wing.

Such wings are usually made from a small roundish feather like the neck and back feathers of a Partridge. These are prepared in the same way as the duck breast feathers used for our Mayflies, except of course that the triangular portion left is very much smaller to produce a wing which will be in proportion to the size of hook used.

Having wound on the bed as usual place the feathers together bright sides inwards so that they fan out in the same way as the Mayfly. Hold the pair of feathers firmly with the right hand and place them on the bed with the stems pointing to the *rear* of the hook. Extend the hold of the thumb and finger to embrace the shank to keep the wing in position. With the other hand tie down these stems with a couple of tight turns of silk.

Lift the wing to the rear and take another turn of silk in front of the wing to "cock" it up. Secure it with a half-hitch then take another turn of silk horizontally round the base of the wing as you did for the English dry fly.

Divide the wings carefully with the dubbing-needle and tie with a figure-of-eight, again as you did for the English dressing, once again being careful not to draw this too tight or the wings will splay out too much. Trim off the waste stubs.

Hackle feathers stripped as for Mayfly

Dry Fly Wing. American style

COMMON FAULTS IN WINGING

(a) Wings of wrong size for the fly in question.
(b) Wing segments of unequal width.
(c) Wings twisted to one side, usually due to failure to provide a "bed".
(d) Wings breaking or splitting.
(e) Dry fly wings splayed out too much.
(f) Wings not springing from the shank at the same angle.
(g) "Spent" wings inclined above or below the horizontal plane.

9

VARIOUS OTHER TECHNIQUES

This chapter covers a few techniques and processes which do not fall conveniently under any of the headings previously dealt with. They do not necessarily bear any relation to each other.

THE USE OF DEER HAIR
This is an American development for which fly-dressers elsewhere should be duly grateful!

The hair from the flank and belly of the American White-tail Deer is coarse and stiff and by the nature of its construction has excellent floating capabilities. Hair from our own Roe or Fallow Deer has much the same qualities.

It is used primarily for the bodies of floating flies and for the characteristic "head" of the "Muddler Minnow", one of the most popular lures in use today. The hair is applied as a dense covering which is then clipped short to give a stiff "brush" effect. Perhaps this is best illustrated by a description of the making of a "Muddler" head:

Assume that the body and wing of the "Muddler" has been tied and trimmed and that there is a space of just over a quarter of an inch between the wing-root and the eye where the head is to be formed.

From a piece of Deer hide with the hair attached cut off a tuft of hair about $\frac{1}{8}$-inch in diameter. Cut this close to the skin and brush the base of the tuft thoroughly to get rid of any fluffy undercoat.

Push this tuft lengthwise over the eye of the hook and hold it in position just in front of the wing, taking a turn of the tying-silk round it. As you draw this taut do not hold the tuft too tightly with the other hand and you will find that the hair will then fan out round the shank as an even "collar".

Wet the tips of the left thumb and finger and pull all the projecting fibres to the rear, then take another tight turn of silk immediately in front of them. Now with the fingernails or the back of a knife push this towards the rear, which will pack the hair down tight.

Take another tuft of the same size and tie this in the same way, packing it hard again. Repeat this with further tufts of hair until the space between the wing and just short of the eye has been filled with a dense collar of hair.

In the case of the "Muddler" you can now wind the head, whip-finish and varnish, but if you are making a body to which wings and hackle are to be added secure the work with a half-hitch.

Using a pair of sharp scissors trim the "head" or body thus formed to the shape you require. You may find it easier to do this if you remove the hook from the vice.

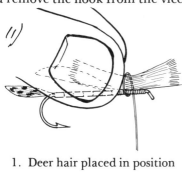

1. Deer hair placed in position

4. Head completed

2. Hair "spun" round shank

5. Whip-finish applied

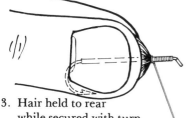

3. Hair held to rear while secured with turn of silk in front

6. Head trimmed

A "Muddler Minnow" head

MULTI-HOOK LURES

On occasion, instead of using a single long-shank hook it may be preferable to use two or more shorter hooks linked together, although some purists regard these with a certain amount of disfavour.

Mounts of this type can be arranged in various patterns:

Both hook-points facing the same way, i.e. in "Tandem".

Two hooks facing opposite ways, as in a "Stewart" tackle.

Three hooks, the middle one set opposite to the other two, like a "Pennell" tackle.

Two-hook lures are sometimes known as "Demons" and those with three as "Terrors". The tail hook is occasionally a double.

If "blind" hooks (i.e. those with a plain shank and no "eye") are used for all but the front hook of the mount it will make a neater job. Eyes can easily be snipped off hooks with pliers or wire-cutters but do be careful to hold the eye away from you when you do this: the last thing you want is a sharp bit of steel in your own eye. The safest way of dealing with an up- or down-eyed hook is to compress the eye in the jaws of a pair of pliers; nearly always it will break cleanly.

To make any of these mounts you will need a length of nylon monofilament; that with a breaking-strain of about eight pounds is usually plenty stout enough. Cut this into three strands about nine inches long and tie these together at one end with an ordinary thumb-knot.

Turn the head or barrel of the vice towards you, clamp the knot firmly in the jaws and plait the monofil strands together (left over centre, right over centre, left over centre and so on) for about two inches; the plait should be regular and tight.

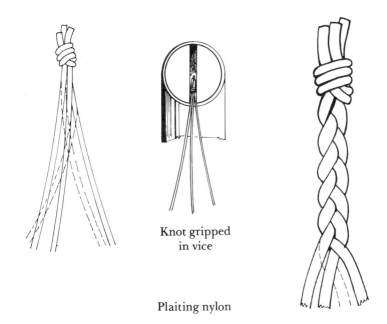

Knot gripped
in vice

Plaiting nylon

Pull the plaited portion hard to straighten it, tie another knot to prevent it unravelling and trim off the spare ends. Remove the plait from the vice, the head of which should be restored to its normal position.

Place a "blind" hook in the vice and run on the tying-silk in close-butted turns to the tail end of the shank, leaving the silk hanging under tension. Smear the upper surface of this whipping with a good adhesive (thinly) and then lay the length of plaited monofil along it with the knot just clear of where the silk whipping ended.

Now whip the monofil down to the shank in tight close-butting turns. There will be a tendency for the plait to roll away clockwise as you whip it so give it an occasional pull towards you to keep it straight along the top of the shank. When you reach the front end of the hook make a neat whip-finish, being careful of the protruding strand of plait. Snip off the knot at the tail as close to the shank as possible.

When the adhesive is dry, coat the whole whipping with varnish, allow this to dry and then remove the hook from the vice.

Place another hook in the vice (an eyed hook if this is to be the front hook of the mount), whip this from head to tail and smear with adhesive as before.

Pick up the previous hook with the plait attached to it and place the plait along the sticky whipping so that there is a gap of about a quarter of an inch or so between the head of the after hook and the tail of the leading one.

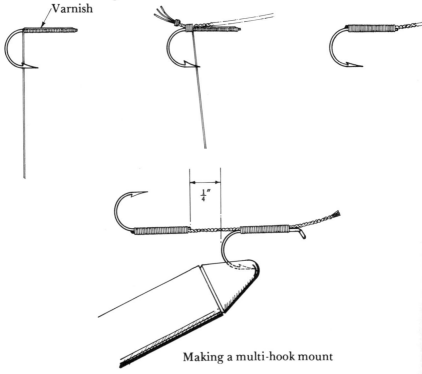

Making a multi-hook mount

Whip the plait down in close-butting turns as before, again avoiding twisting, up to about an eighth of an inch from the eye of the leading hook and whip-finish again. Trim off the waste plait from the front of this hook as close as possible to the shank and varnish this second whipping.

Mounts of this type can be used for Worm Flies or lures of all kinds, using either feathers or hair for the wings.

The dressing can be applied to the completed mount or put on each successive hook as the plait is whipped to it.

Some dressers prefer to use a single thicker strand of nylon, but this tends to kink or twist in use. Others recommend the use of the twisted steel or brass wire used for making up Pike traces. Unless however you happen to be blessed with the gift of a very smooth casting action you will probably find that mounts of such material will kink at the first cast and break in half at the second.

DOUBLE AND TREBLE HOOKS

Again the purist may look on these with some distaste but they have two advantages. They give a more secure hold and there is still the chance of the angler remaining in business if the point of one leg of the hook gets broken.

The basic methods of dressing are the same as for the single hook but there are a couple of things to bear in mind. Only one leg can be put in the vice which means that the plane of the upper surface of the shank is slanted over. If the head or barrel of the vice can be rotated and clamped it is easy to adjust accordingly but if it is of the fixed type you must allow for the fact that the hook is on the slant.

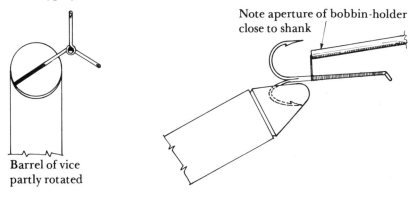

Note aperture of bobbin-holder close to shank

Barrel of vice
partly rotated

The other point is that however carefully you mask the point of the leg in the vice there is another one just outside which is equally ready to catch and snag the tying-silk. The use of a tubular bobbin-holder (see p. 21) will make it easier to work the silk under this exposed point, particularly when dealing with the very small sizes used for trout.

TUBE FLIES
These came into use in the 1950's and while they are extensively used for salmon they are equally effective in the smaller sizes for trout.

The basic principle is that the dressing, which often follows closely that for the more orthodox flies, is tied round a short piece of tube. The cast or leader is then passed through this tube and tied to a treble hook of appropriate size. When a fish is hooked the tube (theoretically) slips up the leader out of the way.

The size and material of the tubing used will vary according to requirements. For salmon in deep heavy water where you want to get down to the fish you may need a murderous concoction on a comparatively heavy brass tube up to three inches long while at the other end of the scale are tiny flies tied on fine-gauge tube. Hard nylon is the better material for these lighter tube-flies; plastic tends to be too soft.

Cut off a short length of tubing. If metal is used make sure that the ends are reamed and filed absolutely smooth or it will surely chafe and cut through the end of the leader. Nylon or plastic is not so likely to chafe but you can if you wish "twiddle" the ends of the tube in the flame of a match or lighter for a split second to burr or "bell" the ends over to prevent the dressing slipping off. Be careful not to overdo this; these materials melt very rapidly and the tube will distort if kept in the flame.

Find a tapestry needle that fits* closely the bore of the tube. (A tapestry needle is preferable to the ordinary type of sewing needle as it has a short blunt point.) Clamp the needle in the vice by its eye so that it is firmly held and points slightly upwards.

Slip the tube over the needle and push it down until you can just rotate it with the fingers; it must not be too tight to move. This applies particularly to soft nylon or plastic which tends to "bind" when the silk is wound on.

---

* It occasionally happens that you cannot find a needle of the precise size required and the tube slips when any tension is applied to the tying silk. This trouble can sometimes be cured by running a length of thread down the inside of the tube before pushing it on to the needle.

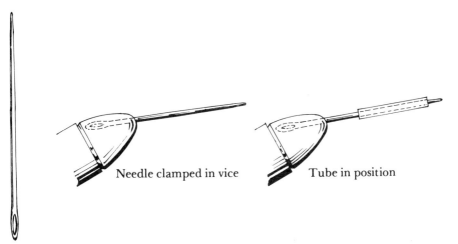

Needle clamped in vice   Tube in position

Tapestry needle. (When obtaining tapestry needles remember that the diameter varies like the "Old" scale for hooks, i.e. the higher the number the thinner the needle.)

Starting about $\frac{1}{8}$-inch behind the front edge of the tube run on the tying-silk and cover the tube with whatever body material you choose, be it floss, tinsel or fur.

At the front end of the tube wind four or five close-butting turns of silk to form a smooth bed for the wing and cover this with varnish. Do not use too much varnish; just enough to make the bed sticky.

Now we come to the wing, which is usually formed from animal hair. Lift from your piece of hide a very small tuft of hair (about a quarter of the total amount you will use for the whole wing), cut this out and brush any undercoat from its base.

Place this tuft on the upper surface of the bed so that the tips of the hairs project well beyond the rear end of the tube and take a turn of tying-silk round it to tie it in. If you do not hold this too tight with your left hand the tuft will spread out a little round the shank.

Rotate the tube on its needle towards you through 90° and tie in a second tuft of hair, the turn of silk holding this falling close-butted to the right of the first turn.

Repeat this two or three times more until the tube is covered with an even dressing of hair, the tips of which should be level. Whip on a couple more tight turns of silk and carefully trim the stubs of hair as close to the wing tie as possible.

Cover these cut ends with more turns of silk to form a neat head.

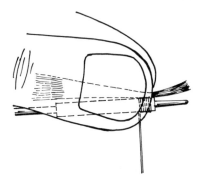

"Positioning" hair

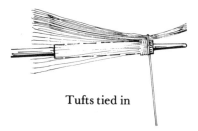

Tufts tied in

Trimmed

Wings for tube-flies can also be made from hackle feathers with long stiff fibres. In this case there will be no need to keep rotating the tube.

Strip the flue from the feather to leave a clean stem and tie this in very securely at the throat. Wind the hackle three or four close turns forward, pick out any caught-up fibres with the dubbing-needle and secure and trim the hackle as for an ordinary collar hackle. Wet the fingers, press the hackle fibres to the rear and secure them with two or three rearwards turns of silk.

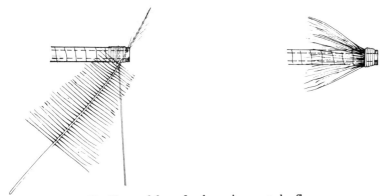

Hackle used for a feather wing on tube fly

*   *   *

VARNISHING THE HEAD
When any fly or lure is completed with a nice neat whip-finished head the last operation is to cover the head with varnish; this not only secures the tie but gives an attractive shiny appearance.

Hold the varnish-bottle and the dubbing-needle upright. Just break the surface of the varnish with the extreme tip of the needle which will give a tiny globule of varnish right on the point of the needle. Still keeping the needle upright apply this drop to the silk and if more is needed repeat the performance. If you slope the needle or dip it in too far you will get too much varnish and it will run where it was not intended.

Be careful to replace the cap on the bottle immediately to avoid evaporation or spilling and wipe the needle clean and dry straight away.

When the varnish is quite dry, always puggle the eye of the fly with a needle to clear out any varnish that might have seeped into it; if you come to change your fly when the light is failing, the wind is getting up and it is starting to rain you may well wish that you had remembered to do this!

Showing the important point of only the tip
of the needle entering the varnish

PART III

PRACTICAL WORK

10

SOME TYPICAL TROUT FLIES

Having duly practised the processes for making the various components of a fly or lure, the novice dresser can now try his skill at combining certain of these processes in order to produce actual flies.

Half a dozen well-known and popular flies have been chosen as examples and these should give most of the guidance required for the tying of flies the dressing of which calls for similar components. After this, it should only be a matter of looking up the "recipe" or dressing in the appropriate reference book. (See Chapter 14.)

Quite apart from their "training" value the examples given are all proven fish-catchers and will all be useful additions to your fly-box when you go fishing.

Example 1
HACKLED WET FLY. "BLACK AND PEACOCK SPIDER."
Materials required:
    Down-eyed hook, fairly short shank, size 12 or smaller.
    Black tying-silk
    Peacock herl, three or four strands.
    Small hen hackle dyed black.

Place the hook in the vice, shank sloping slightly upwards and with the point masked by the jaws of the vice. Flick it with the finger to check that it is securely held.

Load the spool of tying-silk into the bobbin-holder and, starting about ⅛-inch from the commencement of the eye, run-on the silk as taught in "Starting" (see Chapter 5) as far as a spot on the shank opposite the hook-point. Leave the silk hanging down kept taut by the weight of the bobbin-holder. (If you are using a length of silk without a bobbin-holder clip on the heavier pair of hackle-pliers to provide this weight.)

Take the strands of Peacock herl, level them up, and hold them with the left hand about three quarters of an inch from their bases. Place the butts of the herls thus held underneath the shank of the hook, to the right of and touching the dangling tying-silk, with the butts of the herls pointing forwards and upwards.

Holding the bunch of herls firmly with the left hand, with the right bring up the silk keeping it very taut and pass it over the shank in a clockwise direction to "trap" the ends of the herls. Take another turn of silk in the same way to make the hold secure and trim off the stubs of herl about a quarter of an inch from where they are tied-in. Wind the silk back up the shank to just short of where you originally started at the head end, binding down the cut ends of herl close to the shank, and leave the silk hanging (under tension) again. Twist the herls together clockwise and hold the ends together with the right hand to prevent them unravelling. Keeping the twisted strands taut wind them clockwise up the shank in neat turns, each turn butting closely against its predecessor.

When you reach the hanging tying-silk keep the ends of the twisted strands of herl taut and slightly forward (i.e. to your right) and with the other hand bring the silk up and over the shank, keeping it taut, to trap the ends of the herl. Whip on two more close-butted turns of silk towards the eye to secure the body, let the waste ends of herl unravel and either break them off with a flick of the fingers or cut them off close to the shank. Leave the silk hanging under tension again.

Select a good quality black hen hackle with web fibres of the appropriate length (approximately the distance between the eye of the hook and its point) and carefully strip away the flue from its base until you reach nice clean web. Draw the hackle through the fingers to make the web fibres stand out.

With the left hand place the stripped base of the quill under the shank pointing forwards and upwards. The place on the quill where the remaining web starts should be touching and to the right of the dangling silk, the plane of the web should be perpendicular to the shank and the "bright" or outer side of the hackle should face toward the eye.

Hold the hackle very firmly in this position and with the other hand bring the silk up taut over the shank to trap the quill. If the quill tends to roll round the shank unwind that last turn of silk and start again, this time holding everything a little tighter.

Take another taut turn of silk, this time passing it behind the "webbed" part of the hackle (on your side of the hook) and in front of the stripped stem (on the far side). The stem should now be held firmly in position by a neat "figure-of-eight" of tying-silk.

Leaving the silk hanging under tension again, take hold of the webbed end of the hackle. If you do this with the hackle-pliers make sure that the jaws of the pliers are biting down on the central quill and not on the web fibres. Holding the hackle taut all the time wind it in neat touching turns towards the eye; two or three turns are ample for a fly of this type.

Holding the end of the hackle slightly forwards take a couple of turns of silk clockwise through the hackle where the latter is wound round the shank. The silk should be kept taut and "swung" backwards and forwards as it passes through the projecting fibres of the hackle. If this is done those projecting fibres will not be flattened and the silk will bite down securely on the turns of the quill of the hackle. Pick out with the dubbing-needle any hackle fibres that may have got caught up.

When the hackle is securely held, snip off as close to the shank as possible the stub of the quill and the waste end of the web.

Moisten the fingers and stroke all the projecting hackle fibres towards the rear of the hook and cover the cut ends with another turn or two of silk. Wind on half a dozen more turns of silk to form a neat "head" for the fly and finish it off with an equally neat "whip-finish" (see Chapter 5). This should be just clear of the beginning of the eye. Break or cut off the tying-silk right up flush with the head.

Finally, holding the dubbing-needle vertical dip its extreme tip into the varnish and apply a minute drop to the head of the fly, working it well into the turns of silk. With the fingers pull the hackle fibres back into position as a nice evenly wound collar or "ruff" and allow the varnish to dry before putting the fly in your box. Don't forget to clear any varnish from the eye.

Example 2
HAIRWING STREAMER LURE. "SWEENEY TODD"
Materials required:
  Long-shank hook, size 6 or 8.
  Black tying-silk.
  Round or oval silver tinsel (fine).
  Black floss-silk.
  Magenta fluorescent ("D.F.M.") wool or floss.
  Large cock hackle dyed scarlet.
  Grey Squirrel tail or Bucktail, dyed black.

First, check that the hook is firmly held in the vice; there is considerably more "leverage" with hooks of this type.

Run the tying-silk down the shank to opposite the hook point.

Cut off about six inches of tinsel and holding the end firmly with one hand pull the end of the wire covering and fray out the silk core for about ¼-inch. Tie this frayed end in firmly at the rear end of the shank then wind the silk back up the body to a point about ¼-inch short of the original starting place.

Cut off about nine inches of black floss and if it is of the two-strand type separate the strands. Draw one strand several times through the fingers to straighten and flatten it and then tie in one end of it where the silk is hanging at the forward end of the body. Leaving the tying-silk hanging, wind the floss down to the tail and back again, flattening the filaments of floss into a flat "ribbon" rather than a round "cord". If you wish to taper the body add more backwards and forwards turns where you want to thicken it up. Secure the floss with a couple of tight turns of tying-silk and trim off the waste.

Take a complete turn of the tinsel round the shank at the rear end of the body and then continue winding it up the body in even open spiral turns about ⅛-inch apart. It is advisable to wind this tinsel "ribbing" in the reverse direction to that in which the body floss was wound, i.e. if you wound the floss in a clockwise direction wind the tinsel anti-clockwise. Keep these ribbing turns evenly spaced and well apart; many people tend to get these too close together.

Hold the tinsel firmly at the front end and take a firm turn of tying-silk over it. Then cut off the tinsel leaving just under a quarter of an inch protruding. Fray out this protruding end by pulling the wire covering as before and then whip down the silk core. This will hold the tinsel ribbing securely.

Wind the tying-silk forward for about half the distance between the front end of the body and the eye of the hook and tie in a short piece of the magenta fluorescent material. Wind this back to the front end of the body and back again to make a narrow thorax or collar, secure it with the tying-silk and trim off. Note: Fluorescent material is very garish and vivid stuff so be careful not to "overdo" it.

As already mentioned, tying a "false" hackle is much easier if the hook is removed from the vice and replaced upside-down. Remember to rotate the hook towards you as you do this or you will unwind half a turn of the tying-silk.

Select a large cock hackle dyed scarlet, remove any flue, and draw it through the fingers to make the web stand out. Separate off a bunch of web fibres, get their tips level and holding the bunch by the tips rip the quill away. With the finger and thumb of the right hand "position" this at the throat of the hook, if necessary adjusting it with the aid of the other hand (see page 84). The points of the hackle fibres should reach just beyond the point of the hook.

Transfer the hold to the left finger and thumb as already taught and bring the tying-silk up taut between the tips of the left thumb and finger on the "home" side, i.e. between the bunch of fibres and the ball of the left thumb. Nip the silk there to hold it and bring it over and down between the bunch of fibres and the tip of the left finger, i.e. on the "away" side. Draw the silk down steadily vertically to bring the hackle fibres down on to the shank. Take four or five more close turns of silk to secure the hackle and to provide a "bed" for the wing. Trim off the stubs of hackle with a cut sloping towards the eye.

Remove the hook from the vice again and replace it right way up, remembering to avoid unwinding. Place a generous drop of varnish on the bed on the upper surface of the shank where the wing is to be tied.

Lift from the piece of Bucktail or Squirrel a tuft of the long hairs and get the tips of these level; the tuft should be about as thick as a pencil lead. Cut this tuft off close to the skin and holding it firmly in the middle brush out thoroughly any fluffy undercoat; you only want the long "guard" hairs for your wing.

With the right hand position the bunch of hair so that its tips project beyond the bend of the hook for about half the overall length of the hook and transfer the hold to the left hand.

Bring up the silk between the tips of the left thumb and finger on the "home" side, nip it there and bring it down again vertically on the "away" side. Repeat this with two or three more turns of silk then check that the wing is in its correct position. If it is, lift the wing forward and take a complete (360°) turn of tying-silk horizontally round the wing-root. Now wind a couple more perpendicular turns rearwards to cover this "locking" turn.

Trim the stubs of hair with a cut sloping to the eye as you did with the false hackle and then cover these cut ends with several turns of silk to make a neat conical head. Whip-finish and varnish the head.

Example 3

WINGED WET FLY. "MARCH BROWN"
Materials required:

Medium-shank down-eyed hook, size 10 or smaller.
Brown tying-silk.
Bronze speckled shoulder feather from a Mallard drake.
Gold wire (fine gauge).
Fur from a Hare's poll.
Pair of matched (right and left) wing secondary feathers from a hen Pheasant.
Small speckled brown feather from back of an English (or "Grey") Partridge.

Clamp the hook in the vice and run the silk down to the usual place opposite the point. "Close-butting" is not necessary except for the last half dozen turns.

Pull off three or four fairly long fibres from the bronze Mallard shoulder feather, "position" the bunch on top of the shank at the tail end and if satisfactory tie-in as an upswept tail about one and a half times the length of the body.

Take about six inches of gold wire and about $\frac{1}{8}$-inch from one end "nick" or kink it with the fingernails; this will prevent it pulling out. Hold this very firmly with the left hand and tie it in under the shank at the rear end of the body. Lift it out of the way for the time being.

From the Hare's poll nip off with the fingernails a few pinches of the short gingery fur. Place these on a tin-lid or other flat receptacle and tease the fibres apart thoroughly with the dubbing-needle.

Holding the tying-silk very taut with the left hand pick up a small pinch of the teased-out fur with the thumb and finger of the right and then "twiddle" or roll this on to the silk with a clockwise roll. Press hard as you roll and release the pressure at the end of each roll. This should cover the silk with a thin even coating of fur for about an inch. (There is no need to wax the silk for this "dubbing"; a soft fur such as Hare will adhere without it.)

Wind the dubbed silk up the body in neat close clockwise turns, leaving plenty of room at the front end for the wings and hackle. Nip off any excess dubbing with the fingernails.

Holding the gold wire taut take a complete turn with it anti-clockwise round the base of the tail and continue these ribbing turns in a neat spiral about $\frac{1}{8}$-inch apart. Secure the wire firmly at the head end and trim off the waste.

Carefully strip the flue from a small speckled brown Partridge feather and draw it through the fingers to make the fibres stand out, leaving a small triangular tip. Tie this tip in under the shank at the head end with a firm "figure-of-eight". The bright side of the feather should face the eye.

Using either the fingers or the hackle-pliers to hold the stem, wind this hackle three or four close turns forward and then secure it with a couple of turns of tying-silk "swung" through the projecting fibres. Trim out the waste tip and stem.

Divide the hackle fibres on top of the shank and with moistened fingers bring all the hackle below the shank and sloping to the rear. Hold them in this position while you secure them with three or four turns of silk, which will also provide the necessary bed for the wing.

Take the matched pair of hen Pheasant secondaries (choose nicely marked feathers) and strip away all the flue from their bases until good "clean" web is reached. Mark off and cut out a matching segment from each, between $\frac{1}{8}$-inch and $\frac{1}{4}$-inch wide according to the size of hook used. Place one segment exactly over the other, "dull" sides inwards.

Pick up the wing thus formed and with the thumb and finger of the right hand place it in position on top of the bed with the concave curve downwards. The tip of the wing should reach just beyond the bend of the hook.

When you are satisfied with the position of the wing extend the hold of the right finger and thumb to take in the actual shank. This should prevent the wing segments moving as you proceed to the next step, which is to take hold first of the shank and then of the wing segment with the thumb and finger of the left hand. Now release the right.

Holding the wing firmly in position with the left hand, bring up the silk (taut) with the right; pass it between the tips of the left thumb and finger and guide it between the ball of the thumb and the "home" side of the wing. Nip the silk there and then bring it over and down between the "away" side of the wing and the inside of the finger. Draw the silk down steadily vertically so that the base of the wing collapses down on the bed in a "concertina" fold without twisting over to one side.

Repeat this movement twice more, then release the left hand and check that the wing is sitting straight on top of the body in its proper position. If it is not, unwind the turns of silk, scrap the wing and start again with a fresh pair of segments. If it is satisfactory whip on a couple more turns of silk, lift the stub or waste end of the wing and trim it off close to the tie.

Cover this cut end with a few more turns of silk to form a neat head, whip-finish and varnish and you have a very useful addition to your fly-box.

Example 4
"ROLLED" WING DRY SEDGE. "CINNAMON SEDGE"
Materials required:
    Medium shank up-eyed hook, size 12 or smaller.
    Brown tying-silk.
    Fine-gauge gold wire.
    Turkey tail feathers, cinnamon colour.
    Ginger cock hackles.
    Cinnamon brown hen wing secondary feather.

Run the silk to the tail end of the hook, "nick" the end of the gold wire and tie it in.

Select a ginger cock hackle of the appropriate size, strip away the flue, draw it through the fingers leaving a tip of about half an inch or so and tie this tip in under the shank at the tail end.

Take two or three nice long fibres from the cinnamon Turkey tail and tie these in by their butts at the tail next to the hackle tip. Return the silk to the front end, binding down the hackle tip and the butts of Turkey tail. Remember to leave plenty of room at the head.

Twist the Turkey tail fibres together, wind them neatly up the body, secure them and trim off the waste.

Take hold of the ginger hackle that was tied-in at the tail end and wind this in a narrow spiral up the body (clockwise). Keep this taut all the time, with its bright side towards the eye. Secure it at the front end and trim off the waste stub.

Rib this evenly in an anti-clockwise direction with the gold wire, secure and trim. (Ribbing in the reverse direction from the lay of the hackle not only renders the ribbing more visible but strengthens the dressing.) "Swing" the wire through the hackle fibres as you do with the tying-silk and pick out any caught-up fibres with the dubbing-needle.

Mark off a segment about half an inch wide from the web of a single cinnamon brown hen secondary feather. Stroke this out as perpendicular to the quill as possible so that the tips of the individual web fibres are level and cut or strip this segment from the quill.

Place this segment bright side downwards on a flat surface and with the needle or tweezers fold one third of it up and over on to the remainder. Fold the opposite edge over similarly and you should have a strip of wing one third of its original width and three times as thick.

"Position" this on the bed with the "open" edge downwards. The points of the wing can protrude beyond the bend of the hook somewhat further than is usual for wet flies and it should lie fairly flat along the shank to imitate the "roof" shaped wing of a Sedge.

Tie the wing in this position as in the previous example and trim away the stub.

Prepare another stiff ginger hackle of the right size and tie this in by its stem at the throat of the fly. Wind this three or four close turns to give a neat collar hackle immediately in front of the wing-root. Finish off as usual.

Example 5
"UPWINGED" DRY FLY. "OLIVE QUILL"
Materials required:
> Medium shank up-eyed hook, size 12 or preferably smaller.
> Olive tying-silk.
> Cock hackles dyed olive, large and small.
> Peacock herl, dyed olive.
> Matched (right and left) pair of Starling wing feathers, as pale as possible.

Run the tying-silk to the tail in close-butting turns.

From a fairly large olive-dyed cock hackle pull off three good stiff fibres and tie these in above the shank as a tail about half to three quarters of an inch long. Try to spread these fibres out and if you like them cocked up lift them forward and take a turn of silk immediately behind them.

Take a good strand of Peacock herl, put it on a flat surface and strip off the fluffy fibres with short strokes with a piece of india-rubber to leave a clean quill stem. Dyeing Peacock herl has very little apparent effect on this fibre but it does colour the actual quill. Tie this strand of quill in under the shank at the tail.

Wind the tying-silk back in close-butting turns to where the wing is to be tied-in, neatly covering the butt ends of the tail and the quill, and you should now have a smooth slim underbody of tying-silk. Be particularly careful to leave yourself plenty of room at the head end.

Now wind the stripped Peacock herl in neat touching turns up to the tying-silk. Hold the end of the herl taut while you secure it with a couple of turns of silk and then trim off.

Prepare a small olive-dyed cock hackle and tie this in under the shank at the front end. See that all of this remains below the shank as you do not wind it on at this stage.

Take equal segments just over $\frac{1}{8}$-inch wide from the matching pair of Starling wing feathers. Place one exactly over the other, convex sides inwards. It will now be seen that when these are held by the base the segments will curve away from each other.

Position the pair of segments on the bed butts foremost with the concave curve of the wing upwards (the reverse of the wet fly) and tie them down with three turns of silk as you did the wet fly wing in Example 2. Lift the wing forward and take another tight turn of silk immediately behind the wing root to cock the wing upright. Trim out the waste butts of the wing.

To avoid slipping or displacement of the wing during the next operation it is advisable to secure the work at this stage with a half-hitch. Make a small loop in the spare end of the tying-silk and pass this down over the eye to where the work is to be secured and draw it tight.

Now very carefully take a complete 360° clockwise turn of silk horizontally round the base of the wing immediately above the shank; be careful not to pull this too tight or you may distort the wing. Tie another half-hitch here if you so wish.

Gently ease the wings apart with the shank of the dubbing-needle.

Bring the silk up immediately behind the "home" side wing, pass it between the wings, and down immediately in front of the "away" side wing. Bring it round again, this time in front of the home side, between them again, and down behind the away side. You have thus taken a "figure-of-eight" through the wing; again be careful not to pull this too tight or the wings will spread out too much. Take another tight turn of silk round the shank behind the wing and bring it round in front of the wing ready to secure the hackle in due course.

Take hold of the small hackle already tied-in and wind it three or four close turns behind the wing, then bring it in front of the wing and wind a couple more turns. Secure it with the tying-silk and trim off.

Wet the fingers and draw the wing and hackle carefully out of the way while you wind the head, whip-finish and varnish.

Pull the wings and hackle back into shape before the varnish sets.

When you can tie a workmanlike specimen of this on a size 16 hook you can consider yourself a qualified fly-dresser and the making of any fly or lure in this or any other book should hold no terrors for you!

Example 6

"PHEASANT-TAIL NYMPH"

Materials required:

> Down-eyed hook. (The more usual is a medium shank size 12 or 14 but they can prove effective tied on a long-shank 10 or 12.)
> Brown tying-silk.
> "Centre" tail feather from a cock Pheasant.
> Fine gauge gold wire.
> Fine gauge soft copper wire.

Run the silk down the shank as usual.

If you want your nymph to sink quickly, tie in a length of soft copper wire and wind this tightly up and down the shank to give a weighted underbody; otherwise omit this step. (Remember to keep weighted and unweighted varieties in separately labelled compartments in your box.)

Take three nice long fibres from the Pheasant tail and tie these in on top of the shank to make a tail about half an inch long, spreading it if possible. Do not trim off the waste butts at this stage.

Nick the end of a short piece of gold wire, tie this in under the shank at the tail and push it out of the way for the time being. Lift the stubs of Pheasant tail and wind the silk back halfway up the body.

Now hold the three untrimmed butts of herl together and wind them in neat close turns up to the silk, where they should be secured and trimmed off.

Rib neatly with the gold wire and secure and trim that.

Take a bunch of exactly six more tail fibres and tie these in by their points above the shank at the halfway mark. Their butts should point to the rear and their bright sides should be downwards.

Take another bunch of four or five similar fibres and tie these in by their points underneath the shank immediately below the previous six fibres. Again the butts should point to the rear.

Trim off the waste points of all these fibres level with the start of the eye of the hook, Wind the silk forward again to just short of the eye.

Take hold of the bunch of fibres tied underneath the shank, twist them together and wind them in close turns forward to make a bulky "thorax". Secure and trim off.

Now take the six fibres tied on top of the shank and bring them over and forward over the thorax to represent the elytra or wing-cases of the insect. The bright side of the fibres should now show on the upper surface. Tie these down firmly with the tying-silk but do not trim the ends off yet.

Divide these ends three and three either side of the hook and whip them down with a "figure-of-eight" of silk to make them stick out horizontally.

Form the head and whip-finish and then trim these projecting "legs" to about quarter of an inch long.

11

SALMON FLIES

The traditional "fully-dressed" salmon-fly was a real masterpiece of craftsmanship and like everything else that involves time, patience and skilled workmanship it has tended of recent years to give place to more simple (and possibly equally effective) patterns that can be turned out much more quickly and cheaply.

I have included in this chapter some notes on the making of these traditional forms, not only for the sake of those who still prefer to use them but because the tying of such flies is a challenging exercise and there is great satisfaction to be derived from the completion of a good specimen.

Some of the patterns are very ornate and whether you would be prepared to risk losing or breaking one in use is another matter, although they are doubtless attractive to salmon. Even if the hook does get broken such a fly makes a handsome hat-ornament, indeed some enthusiasts tie them as brooches.

As regards this extra ornamentation, the bodies of these flies are often complicated combinations of fur, floss and tinsel and in addition to "tags" and "butts" (see pp. 74 & 75) the junction of these body materials may be covered with a fan-shaped spray of short feather fibres. This is what is meant by body *veiling*.

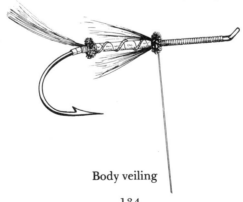

Body veiling

134

It is when we come to look at the wings that things really get complicated. Some of these are *built* up of several layers:

First, an *underwing*, possibly of Turkey tail or Golden Pheasant tippet.

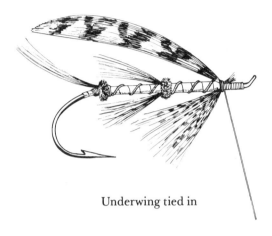

Underwing tied in

This is then almost covered by a composite or "married" wing, consisting of three or more strips of feather of different colour or even species joined together (see page 98).

"Married" wing tied over underwing

In turn this is again almost covered by a *veiling* wing, usually of some thin feather such as Mallard or Teal shoulder.

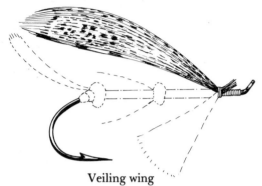

Veiling wing

The wing is sometimes finished off by adding a *"topping"* along the top of it, usually a long Golden Pheasant crest feather. The bright gold of this gives a lovely overall "halo" effect.

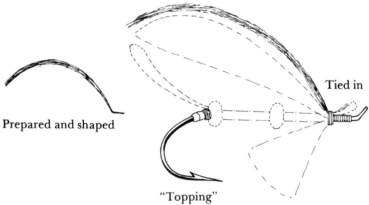

Prepared and shaped

Tied in

"Topping"

The fly can be further adorned with *sides* or *cheeks* made of slips of brightly coloured feather such as Scarlet Ibis or Kingfisher.

Eyes, tied in at the root of the wing, were formed from the spectacular "enamelled" feathers from the neck of a Jungle Cock (see Chapter 12). This is now virtually unobtainable but it is possible to buy plastic substitutes; my own reaction is that these look as horrible as they sound.

Some old dressings also call for *horns*, which are two long fibres from the tail of a Macaw springing out from the shoulder of the fly, but these are rarely encountered nowadays.

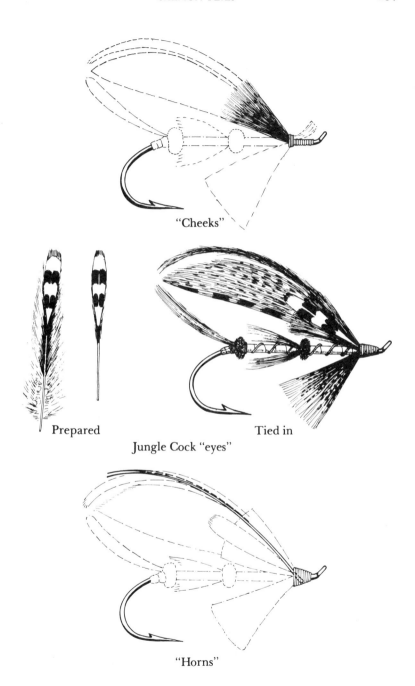

"Cheeks"

Prepared   Tied in

Jungle Cock "eyes"

"Horns"

Once again, we will start by tackling something comparatively simple and straightforward, a "Low water" pattern.

This type of fly is for use when the river is low and clear. The hooks on which they are dressed are quite light in the wire and the dressing appears very sparse and small for the size of hook used. The general idea seems to be that if a fish snaps at the dressing of the fly he will get the business end of the hook as well.

Example 7
"SILVER BLUE"
Materials required:
    Low-water salmon hook; size 4 is usually big enough.
    Black tying-silk, "Gossamer" or "Naples".
    Golden Pheasant crest feather.
    Flat silver tinsel (medium width).
    Round or oval silver tinsel (medium).
    Hen hackle dyed bright blue.
    Teal drake shoulder feathers (black and white bars).

Starting about halfway down the eye-bar, run on the tying-silk in close-butting turns down to a point only about halfway down the shank.

Strip the flue from the base of the Golden Pheasant crest feather, which should then be tied in as an up-curving tail about $\frac{3}{4}$-inch long.

Fray out the end of the piece of round or oval silver tinsel and tie this in underneath the shank under the tail.

Wind the tying-silk carefully back in close-butting turns to just short of your original starting-point.

Tie in here the flat silver tinsel and wind this down to the tail in neat touching but not overlapping turns. Wind this neatly back to where the silk is hanging and holding the end taut whip a couple of turns of silk forward over it. Bend the end of the tinsel back flat over these turns and whip on a couple more turns to the rear, which will hold the tinsel securely. Waggle the end of the tinsel until it breaks off.

Tie-in and wind on the blue hackle, keeping this fairly sparse. Bring all the fibres below the shank and check that the usual bed of silk is formed.

Take equal segments about $\frac{3}{16}$-inch wide from a matched pair of

Teal shoulder feathers and place these exactly together bright sides outwards to form the wing. Alternatively take a segment just over half an inch wide from a single feather and fold this into three to produce a "rolled" wing.

Tie-in the wing so that its tip only just reaches beyond the root of the tail.

Example 8
"FULLY DRESSED" SALMON FLY. "SILVER DOCTOR"
There are slight variations as between one writer and another for the exact detail of the dressings of these old patterns but the dressing given below fulfils most of the requirements.
Materials required:

Normal pattern salmon hook, any size.

Black Naples tying-silk.

Round or oval silver tinsel (fine or medium grade according to size of hook).

Yellow floss-silk.

Golden Pheasant crest.

Scarlet wool.

Flat silver tinsel (medium width).

Cock hackle dyed bright blue.

Teal or Wigeon black and white barred shoulder feather (medium).

Golden Pheasant "tippet" feathers.

Golden Pheasant tail.

Paired Swan or Goose wing secondaries, dyed scarlet, yellow and blue.

Pale mottled Turkey wing or tail.

Paired Mallard bronze speckled shoulder feathers, (large).

Paired Teal shoulder (black and white) (large).

Large Golden Pheasant crest for "topping".

First, take the big Golden Pheasant "topping" and wet it thoroughly, then put it down flat on a piece of glass or similar shiny flat surface, shaping it to fit the size of the finished fly. Kink or crimp the stem at the point where it will ultimately be tied-in and leave it to dry and set.

Now run-on the silk in close-butting turns to the tail end.

Fray and tie-in the round tinsel, wind the silk forward a few turns, wind the tinsel about three close turns to make a "tag" and secure it. Do not trim off the tinsel at this stage; the loose end will be wanted for ribbing later.

Tie-in a short strand of yellow floss, wind this as a second tag in front of the silver, secure it and trim off.

Tie-in the short Golden Pheasant crest feather as an up-curving tail.

Tie-in a short piece of well teased-out scarlet wool and wind this a couple of turns to make a butt. (See that the loose end of the round tinsel runs underneath this.)

Take the blue hackle by its tip and draw it through the fingers, then tie it in by its tip in front of the butt.

Return the tying-silk to the front end, allowing plenty of room for the wings and hackle.

Tie in here a length of flat silver tinsel, wind this down to the butt in neat touching turns and back to the forward end, where it should be secured and trimmed.

Rib in the reverse direction with the remainder of the round tinsel in wide even turns. Secure and trim.

Hold the blue hackle taut with the left hand, wet it thoroughly and stroke all the projecting fibres back so that they point to the rear. Continuing to hold the hackle taut wind it up the body, the stem of the hackle following immediately behind the turns of ribbing tinsel. Secure it at the front and trim off.

Tie-in a false hackle made from a bunch of fibres from a black and white barred Teal or Wigeon feather.

Now for the winging:

First, take half a dozen or so long fibres from the Golden Pheasant tippet, lay these along the top of the shank and tie them in as a flat underwing.

To make up the main "married" wing start at the lower edge with a narrow strip of Golden Pheasant tail; this is springy and difficult stuff to handle. Above this marry narrow strips of scarlet dyed Goose or Swan, followed by blue then yellow and finally pale Turkey. Build up the opposite wing with strips from the other side of the birds, match up the pair of wings thus made and tie them in.

For the "veiling" wing as it is called take a narrow segment of barred Teal shoulder and marry it to a segment of bronze Mallard of twice the width. On the far side of the Mallard marry on another strip of Teal of the same width as the first. If you now fold this down the middle of the Mallard you should have a "roof" showing equal amounts of Mallard above and Teal below.

Place this over the first wing so that the veiling wing is slightly shorter than the main wing and that the lower edge of the veiling wing just shows the red stripe in the main wing. Tie this in and trim off the stubs.

Hold the "topping" carefully in place along the top of the wing and tie it down. The end of the topping should just touch the end of the smaller crest tied-in as a tail.

Cover the head with a couple of turns of scarlet wool or give it a coat of red varnish.

An alternative way of putting on the wing is as follows:

Make up the two main married wings as before and place them separate on a flat surface, bright sides uppermost.

Instead of making the veiling wing in one piece, make two separate right and left wings.

Near the butts of one main wing spread a drop of varnish. With the tweezers pick up the corresponding veiling wing and press this down on the main wing in the required position.

Repeat this with the other pair of wings, then place both pairs together and tie them in as one wing.

The incriminating evidence of varnish will be removed when the stubs are trimmed off.

"GRUBS"
These are large heavily dressed "palmer"-type flies with little or no wing.

Example 9
"TIPPET GRUB"
Materials required:
    Normal weight salmon hook, single or double, size to taste.
    Black Naples tying-silk.
    Round or oval gold tinsel, medium gauge.
    Seal's fur dyed scarlet.
    Golden Pheasant tippet feathers.
    "Furnace" cock hackles. (Mahogany red with black "list").
    Green wool.
    Round or oval silver tinsel (medium).

Run-on the silk and wind on some gold tinsel to form a narrow tag.

Wax the silk, dub on some scarlet Seal's fur and wind this for a couple of turns to give a second tag.

Tie in a smaller tippet feather and wind this round the shank immediately in front of the fur so that it sticks out all round like a collar. Secure it with the silk so as to slant all the projecting fibres to the rear.

Follow this closely with one turn of a "furnace" hackle of about the same size and secure this in the same way.

Tie-in a strand of green wool and the silver tinsel and then run the silk forward to halfway up the body. Wind the green wool up to it and rib it with the silver tinsel. Do not trim the wool or the tinsel, they will be wanted again shortly.

Tie-in and wind on another tippet and furnace hackle (slightly larger than before) and again slant these to the rear.

Wind the silk forward again to just short of the eye, wind the green wool up to it, rib with the silver tinsel again and secure. Trim the wool but leave the tinsel for the moment.

Tie-in and wind on a third tippet and furnace hackle (again larger), wind two or three turns of the silver tinsel to form the head and finish off as usual.

"DEE" AND "SPEY" FLIES

These generally speaking are big flies for heavy waters and while most of the dressings include a prominent body-hackle of natural or dyed Heron their special characteristic is the manner in which comparatively short wings are tied to lie low and flat.

HAIRWINGS AND TUBE FLIES

As already mentioned these have now largely replaced the old fully-dressed flies as the salmon-fisherman's weapon.

They are merely scaled-up versions of those already referred to in this book and present few problems in the tying. The dressings of the old favourite flies can easily be adapted to these modern forms; many sorts of feather have a counterpart of similar colour in hair (e.g. Teal and Silver Baboon) and paler hair can often be dyed in bright shades.

WADDINGTONS

An alternative to the tube-fly is the lure of the "Waddington" type.

This was invented by Mr. Richard Waddington some thirty odd years ago and many patterns of it are marketed by John Dickson & Co., the successors to Messrs. Alex Martins.

The lure could be described as a fixed or non-sliding tube fly; they are dressed in much the same way as the tube and their basic mounts are not difficult to make.

For these you need some 16-gauge half-hard brass wire, a supply of eyed treble hooks and a pair of pliers with fine round-nosed points. If you have in your workshop a pair of special wire-bender's pliers, the jaws of which terminate in small studs round which the wire is shaped, the job is that much easier.

Cut off about three inches of wire and bend one end over to give a "leg" about half an inch long, forming a neat eye in the angle of the bend. Make another similar eye at the length required for the mount and clip the end of the second leg off so that the two cut ends just meet but do not overlap.

Open one leg and pass the eye of a treble hook of appropriate size down into the loop. Close the leg again and whip the mount with tying-silk or floss to keep it together. If you are handy with a soldering-iron you can of course make a much neater and stronger job by soldering the mount together.

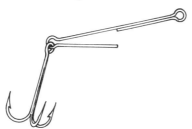

Place in the vice the loop that carries the treble and dress the "shank" of the mount in much the same way as you would a tube. Remember that there will be an exposed treble at the tail of the mount and handle the dressing with care accordingly.

Before attaching the treble hook it is advisable to push a short piece of cycle-valve rubber down over its shank. This can be worked back over the rear eye of the mount when the dressing is completed and will prevent the treble "hingeing".

Any good idea such as the "Waddington" can be relied upon to bring suggestions for improvements from fly-tying enthusiasts and my friend Mr. E. B. Roberts has produced an alternative which to my mind has advantages.

The mount, which is made from lighter gauge stainless steel wire, has the loop which carries the hook formed like an "overhand" knot and if the hook gets broken it can be "worked" off and replaced without damaging the dressing of the lure.

A

The tail of wire at "A" projects slightly and prevents the hook from doubling back on the body, a common objection where lures of this sort are used.

PART IV

FEATHERS AND FUR

12

COLLECTION OF MATERIALS

Many fly-dressers buy their feathers and other materials from suppliers specialising in this trade, several of whom advertise regularly in the angling press.

Because such firms carry large stocks they can offer a wide range of carefully matched material of good quality and their prices are by no means excessive if one pauses to take into account the skill, time and trouble involved in sorting and matching feathers. Sorting through a mixed bag of feathers given to you by a friend or a cheap "job lot" bargain packet should convince you of the accuracy of this statement.

Every project seems to throw up its own particular "spin-off" or subsidiary developments, and the fly-dresser's rising standard of competence as a craftsman will almost certainly be accompanied by a wider understanding of the structure and capabilities of the materials he is using and by an interest in collecting his own stocks.

Moreover, in addition to the interest in entomology engendered by his attempts to fashion as exact imitations as possible of particular insects, his increasing knowledge of natural materials is likely to develop a like interest in ornithology and similar natural sciences.

Here a word of caution may not come amiss. These secondary

interests must remain in their proper perspective otherwise it will be found that the study and collection of the materials is occupying more time than the actual fly-tying, which is of course a self-defeating exercise.

It is very common too for the tyer, particularly the beginner, to amass a quantity of highly decorative materials which are quite useless for practical fly-tying.

Having said this we can now look at this question of collecting materials and the best ways of setting about it.

Our fly-dresser may be fortunate enough to number among his friends poultry-keepers, shooting men or gamekeepers who would be willing to give him feathers, etc. In fact these will frequently be offered to him once his fly-dressing proclivities become known.

The notes that follow may give him some ideas as to what he should ask such friends to save for him:

DOMESTIC POULTRY
While wing secondaries and hackles from hen birds are comparatively easy to obtain in the range of colours required, cock hackles may present a difficulty. As already mentioned in the notes on dry-fly hackles (Chapter 4), most dressers prefer the hackle of a dry-fly to be stiff and springy, but the neck feathers of a domestic cockerel do not usually attain this desirable state until the bird is a couple of years old. In these days such fully matured birds are few and far between and the reason is not far to seek.

With today's ever increasing food and rearing costs to feed a "broiler" bird up to the killing age of nine to ten weeks, by which time its feathers are still soft and not much use for our purpose, it is obviously not economic to continue to feed the bird for another two years at a further considerable cost, at the end of which period the carcase value will show little if any increase and there are no compensating eggs. The professional poultryman will probably look askance at this expensive way of growing mere feathers for a bunch of crazy fishermen!

In fact, most of the "capes" of cock hackles now sold by dealers here are imported from the less-developed areas of Asia and Africa. No doubt as these countries learn to develop and modernise their agricultural methods their poultry producers too will jump on the broiler band-wagon and good quality capes will become difficult to obtain.

This prospect raises the question as to where we are to look for these mature and desirable hackles in the future. One answer appears to be to go in for poultry-keeping ourselves or to cultivate a beautiful friendship with someone else who does so.

Hackles can be taken from an old bird without killing or harming it. In the words of the old cookery-book "first catch your bird" then snip off a few hackles with a pair of scissors. The bird will replace these at the next moult and the fact that they are lacking the base of the stem, which you never use anyway, is unlikely to make any difference from your point of view as a fly-dresser. Care must of course be taken to avoid excessive denuding of one unfortunate bird.

Alternatively, if you know the whereabouts of an old cockerel of the type required ask the owner to save the neck for you as and when the bird is killed.

Provided (and only provided) that you have the space, time and facilities for it, raising your own birds can prove an interesting hobby. If you can breed up a good healthy strain of Game or Bantam fowls you may get some good colours for your collection and if these should include birds with "Greenwell", "Coch-y-bonddu" or similar hackles, keep them out of sight when your fellow fly-dressers come to call.

It must be emphasised that as with any form of livestock poultry are a "tie" and if you want to go for a holiday or even a week-end's fishing you must make proper arrangements for feeding and supervision during your absence. Unless such proper attention can be absolutely guaranteed such a project is best not considered.

Another difficulty for the traditionalist and purist is that the old familiar breeds are becoming scarce. The Rhode Island Red giving the rich mahogany "red" of so many dressings, the Light Sussex giving the "badger" and so many others are now only kept by a few enthusiasts, while the commercial grower only produces hybrid strains with names like "Smith's 234" or "Robinson's 56A" or something equally meaningless to the uninitiated.

OTHER DOMESTIC BIRDS

Other feathers for which you can ask your farmer and poulterer friends will provide welcome and useful additions to your stock. The following list sets out some typical examples, with the uses to which they can be put:

White Duck

The wing feathers are used for wings of "Coachman", etc.

White Goose

The wing secondaries are ideal for dyeing bright colours to build traditional salmon-flies. The smaller shoulder feathers can also be dyed scarlet to provide the substitute for Scarlet Ibis.

Turkey

The fluffy feathers from the inside of the thigh of the white variety, which take dye well, provide the "Marabou" used in many streamer flies and lures. The tails and wing secondaries of this breed are a poor substitute for Goose.

The white-tipped tails of the American Bronze variety are used in certain salmon-flies but it is difficult to find feathers of this type that are not frayed and "tatty".

Wing secondaries, particularly those of the "Oak" or speckled kind used for "Muddler Minnows", are always acceptable.*

Guinea Fowl (or Gallena)

The rounded speckled neck feathers, either left natural or dyed blue, are used as hackles for salmon-flies (e.g. "Thunder and Lightning"). The wing secondaries from a well-marked bird make a "strong" and handsome wing for a trout-fly, but for some reason these seem to be more popular amongst American dressings. They are particularly useful for teaching the beginner.

AVIARY BIRDS

If you or any of your friends keep an aviary much decorative and useful material can come your way. In addition to the "exotics" mentioned later in this Chapter the following are not uncommon; indeed some of them may even be encountered in the wild state in certain areas.

Peacocks

The "eyed" tail feathers provide herls and your coarse-fishing friends will be grateful for the stripped quills for making floats. At the base of the tail are some tapered feathers of unusual form; these are known as the "sword" feathers and make the wings of "Alexandra", etc. The blue neck feathers are used for the "Ilen Blue" and the wing secondaries can be used for certain salmon-flies.

There is an "albino" variant of this bird and dyeing the herls from the tail could open up possibilities.

---

* Owing to the popularity of the white bird for table purposes feathers of the Bronze or Oak variety have become difficult to obtain.

Golden Pheasant (cocks)

This magnificent creature, like the Peacock, could well have been expressly designed with the fly-dresser in mind: he can use almost everything but the squawk!

The golden yellow crest provides small feathers for tails and the longer "toppings" for our salmon-flies.

The orange and black-striped "tippet" feathers from the neck give us tails for "Mallard and Claret", "Peter Ross" and many other old favourites, and the complete feather can be used as a salmon-fly wing ("Durham Ranger", etc.) These tippet feathers have a distinctive black stripe about halfway down; this provides an excellent "marker" when tying them in for a tail.

The red body feathers provide hackles for salmon-flies such as "Lady Caroline" and also go to make up the "General Practitioner".

The scarlet "sword" tails have their place in some salmon-flies (e.g. "Gordon") and the twin centre tails are frequently used in the traditional "built" wing.

Lady Amherst Pheasant (cocks)

Fibres from the magnificent black and white tail are used in some Mayfly dressings and the black and white tippets and scarlet crest give an alternative to those of the Golden Pheasant.

It will be noticed that in the case of the last two species I have referred to the cock bird only; the hens of both are very dowdy little Plain Janes.

Carolina Ducks (or rather drakes!)

Amongst other decorative plumage these have handsome black and white barred shoulder feathers (the "Summer Duck" of the catalogues) which make a nice addition to many salmon-flies.

Mandarin Ducks (drakes)

Some of the plumage of this is very similar to that of the Carolina.

Macaw

Fibres from the long red or blue tail feathers provide the "horns" mentioned in old salmon-fly dressings, but there is little call for these in today's more simplified and utilitarian dressings.

Family Pets

The brightly coloured tail-coverts of the Budgerigar can do duty for the Kingfisher and Blue Chatterer if the appropriate shade is available. The red tail feathers of the Grey African Parrot can also find a home somewhere.

Having dealt with the domesticated birds let us now consider the wild species. Apart from certain pests and those which are the recognised quarry of the game shooter and wildfowler, these are strictly protected by law, and very rightly so.

GAME BIRDS

Taking game and wildfowl first we find many that are very useful to the fly-dresser, and can be obtained from a shooting friend.

Pheasants (cocks)

The tails, particularly the "centres", provide fine herls for "Pheasant-tail Nymph", "Daddy-long-legs" and Mayflies.

The bright copper neck feathers with black tips are used for the "Bracken Clock" and can at a pinch make a substitute for Golden Pheasant tippet.

The "church window" feathers along the back make the wing for the "Houston Gem". Save the little white "ring-neck" feathers to dye as a substitute for Toucan and Indian Crow.

If there are any nice neat greenish feathers towards the rump, try these for a New Zealand lure of the "Mrs Simpson" type.

Pheasants (hens)

The wing-secondaries are strong-fibred feathers and thus an ideal medium for the beginner's practice. They also provide the wings for "March Brown", "Grannom", etc.

The "centre" tails make the wing of the "Invicta".

Patridge (English or Grey)

The silvery speckled neck feathers provide hackles for such favourites as "Partridge and Yellow", and the brown speckled feathers from the back of the neck are used for "March Brown".

The wing secondaries make nice wings for small flies calling for a feather like hen Pheasant.

French Partridge ("Red-legged")

The lavender-grey breast feathers make the hackles of a wet Mayfly. (Use that one on the Test and your invitation won't be repeated!)

The chestnut-brown tail feathers can be used for small "Cinnamon Sedge".

Red Grouse

The speckled wing and tail feathers and the hackles are used in the "Grouse" series of dressings.

Snipe and Woodcock

The small dark grey coverts at the "elbow" of the Snipe are used for the "Snipe and Purple" and the wing secondaries and coverts of the Woodcock give the wings for the "Woodcock" series.

WILDFOWL
Mallard (duck)

While some purists may maintain that it is technically only the drake that should be referred to as a Mallard, for the sake of avoiding confusion I am prepared to commit an Irishism and refer to the female as a Mallard duck.

The wing secondaries are good "strong" feathers and form the wings of several popular flies ("Wickham's Fancy", etc.).
Mallard (drake)

The lovely blue wing feathers are wanted for the "Butcher" and its variations. (Save the white-tipped ends of these for things like "Heckham Peckham", etc.).

The shoulder feathers, one side of which is a rich speckled bronze-brown, are an essential for the fly-dresser. They form the wings of "Mallard and Claret", etc. and in the larger sizes are used for salmon-flies.

The soft grey speckled feathers on the flank make the wings of the "Professor" and can at a pinch be used as a substitute for Teal shoulder.

The small spoon-shaped breast and neck feathers, either natural or dyed, provide the "fan wing" for the Mayfly.
Note: Try to collect your Mallard feathers from birds taken when the winter is well advanced. The bronze shoulder feathers to which I have referred will not be found on a bird in "eclipse" or summer plumage.

Teal (duck)

Use the wing secondaries as for Mallard duck.
(drake)

The black and white barred feathers from the shoulder are invaluable to the fly-dresser. The larger feathers which are so expensive to buy are extensively used in salmon-flies and the smaller sizes, together with the similarly marked feathers from the flank give us the wings of "Peter Ross", "Teal, Blue and Silver" and many other well-known patterns.
Pintail and Wigeon

These too carry some beautiful black and white feathers that can be used in the same way as Teal.

OTHER COMMON BIRDS

Starling
> Wing feathers are useful for the wings of many small wet and dry flies such as "Black Gnat", "Blue Dun", "Greenwell's Glory" etc.

Moorhen
> Wings and tails give a "blae" wing.

Coot
> Wing feathers provide the wing for the "Blue winged Olive".

Jay
> The blue feathers make a spectacular wing and are also useful for hackles of "Invicta", "Connemara Black" and the smaller salmon flies.

Magpie
> The tails make nice shiny "elytra" or wing-cases for beetle imitations.

Rook or Crow
> Wing and tail feathers make a good black wing but tend to be rather brittle in texture.

Jackdaw
> The grey throat feathers give the soft hackles for the "Iron Blue" and some Grayling flies.

Woodpigeon
> So far as I can ascertain, this ubiquitous pest does not even have the merit of being useful to the fly-dresser!

"PROTECTED" BIRDS, (which you may pick up as "casualties").

Barn Owl/Brown Owl
> The wide soft web of the wing feather makes a perfect wing for "wake" flies such as the "Hoolet" moth imitation or the "Murragh" Great Red Sedge.

Heron
> The long straggly hackles are ideal for "Dee" and "Spey" flies, either left natural ("Lady Caroline") or dyed black ("Ackroyd", "Black King" etc.). The wing feathers, with wide web and "strong" fibre, can also prove useful.

Kingfisher
> The small blue feathers form the tail of the "Kingfisher Butcher" and the cheeks of the more decorative salmon-flies.

Swan
> The wing secondaries and coverts are even better than Goose for dyeing.

EXOTIC OR FANCY PLUMAGE

The reader of books on fly-dressing, particularly some of the older classics dealing with the traditional fully-dressed salmon-flies, may come across references to the plumage of certain exotic foreign birds which was at one time incorporated in the dressings.

This, and for this we may be thankful, is no longer used and while admittedly substitutes are not the same thing as the genuine article, serviceable imitations can be turned out once you know the appearance of the real thing.

This would seem to be a logical place to mention some of these items and the notes that follow may help if you visit an aviary of tropical birds or refer to books on the subject.

The first five of these come from much the same part of the world, the forests of northern South America.

Blue Chatterer *(Cotinga nattererii)*
>About the size of a small Thrush, this is mainly a shining turquoise blue with purple throat and breast and black wings.
>
>As an "ersatz" for the turquoise feathers try tail-coverts from a Budgerigar of the same colour.

Cock of the Rock *(Rupicola rupicola)*
>Roughly the size of a Jay, this bird carries on its head an unmistakable crest or hood. The plumage is brilliant orange with black wings and tail and a suggested substitute for the body feathers is the small neck feathers from a white Guinea Fowl dyed to a pinkish orange.

Indian Crow *(Pyroderus scutatus)*
>Most reference books give the Indian Crow as *Corvus splendens.* This is a grey and black bird (with no red feathers on it) which is common in India.
>
>The fly-dresser's "Indian Crow" has nothing to do with India; it is the Red-ruffed Fruit Crow of Colombia and Venezuela, a small black bird with a vivid red head and breast. These red breast feathers used for decorating salmon-flies can be imitated by dyeing the white "ring-neck" feathers from a cock Pheasant.

Scarlet Ibis *(Eudocimus ruber)*
>This is about the size of a Curlew with a uniform coloration of deep scarlet.
>
>Wing-coverts from a white Goose dyed scarlet will provide all the "Butchers" and suchlike that you are likely to want.

Toucan *(Ramphastos dicolorus)*

About the size of a Rook, with a huge banana-like beak, this bird is familiar to most of us from the "Guinness" advertisements.

The orange-yellow breast feathers, used for veiling the bodies of salmon-flies, can again be copied by dyeing the "ring-neck" Pheasant feathers.

The other items sometimes quoted came from India.

Jungle Cock *(Gallus sonnerati)*. See illustration, page 137.

The Grey or Sonnerat's Jungle Fowl inhabits the jungles of India and is slightly smaller than our own domestic fowl. The cock bird is a very handsome fellow, his most striking characteristic being his "cape", which consists of black hackles with a white stripe along the edges and bearing at the tip of each a peculiar orange-yellow "eye" giving the appearance of high-gloss enamel paint. This can no longer be imported legally.

A possible substitute is body feathers from a Starling to which a spot of quick drying paint has been applied. The "correcting fluid" used by typists has also been suggested but neither of these bear comparison with the real thing.

Florican (or Florikan)

This is the Indian Bustard (*Otis aurica*), found in India and the Persian Gulf area.

It is a large bird about the size of a Turkey and is similar to the Great Bustard (*Otis tarda*) which once frequented Salisbury Plain and is still to be found in South-eastern Europe.

While the general overall colour is a sandy brown the wing feathers, which were occasional components of salmon-flies, are barred with darker brown. These would be difficult to copy and the only suggestion is to take a pale Turkey wing feather and mark it with a felt-tipped pen.

ANIMAL HAIR

Having dealt at some length with feathers we now turn our attention to fur, and here are some of the items which could come your way from your shooter and gamekeeper friends.

Deer

Hair from the belly and flank of a Roe or Fallow deer makes excellent "Muddler Minnows" and the speckled brown crest along the back of a Fallow buck is the hair equivalent of bronze Mallard feather.

Hare
  The ears and face show quite a range of colour from ginger to black and the fur from these provides the traditional body material for numerous flies including "Gold ribbed Hare's Ear", "March Brown" and others.
Rabbit
  This is not extensively used but the soft blue-grey undercoat can sometimes take the place of Mole.
Grey Squirrel
  The fly-dresser is one of the few people who have a good word for this pest. The tail is invaluable for hairwing flies of all sorts, the "Muddler Minnow" and tube-flies. If you want fairly short hair take it from the base of the tail, leaving the longer hair at the tip for those lures which call for it.
    It is extraordinarily resistant to dye and if you want it coloured you must use a high concentration; it seems to have a particular antipathy to black dye.
Stoat
  The black tail is ideal for small hairwings and tube-flies.
Mink
  This escapee from fur-farms has assumed the status of a pest in some parts of Britain.
    The soft undercoat dubbed thickly on a short-shanked hook gives a remarkable likeness to a trout-pellet!
Mole
  Either left natural or dyed to a particular shade, this fine soft fur is very easy to dub on to tying-silk even without the aid of wax and makes excellent bodies ("Blue Dun" etc.).
Water Vole
  Another short close fur with good water-resisting qualities. Sometimes misnamed Water Rat, do not confuse this with the common rat, a filthy animal which should under no circumstances be handled.

OTHER "INCIDENTALS"
  Road casualties. These may include the occasional Red Squirrel or Badger. While one deeply regrets the loss of such uncommon and delightful animals the tail of the Squirrel and the long body hair of the Badger make excellent hairwings. You may occasionally be offered the "brush" of a Fox, but this is not really of much use as the hair is too soft and fluffy for most purposes.

Horsehair

This can easily be obtained in a good range of colours and is just the thing for bodies of Chironomids such as the "Footballer".

White horsehair takes dye colours well.

Yellow Labrador Dog

Your dog may be willing to spare the occasional snip from his tail. This was the origin of that well-known hairwing salmon-fly, the "Garry" or "Minister's Dog".

Be careful about trying this on other people's dogs; they or their owners may resent the liberty taken!

"Bought" Hair

Certain varieties of hair, mainly "scrap" from the furriers' trade, are now obtainable from many dealers.

These include Bucktail, a long rather rank hair available either in its natural brown and white or dyed various colours, and many varieties of Squirrel.

Calves' tails can sometimes be obtained from a friendly butcher. Although this is soft hair which tends to cling together in the water it is very easy to use and the white hair takes dye readily.

"SALVAGE"

It is worth while keeping an eye open for any unconsidered trifle that may come in useful. An old Ostrich feather "boa" will provide masses of usable herls and you might even find some Jungle Cock as a hat-trimming.

Finally, never refuse anything that may be offered to you. Even if it is "high", moth-eaten or completely useless accept it with good grace and wait till the donor has gone before consigning it to the dustbin; his next contribution may be just what you were looking for.

You can "educate" your contributors if you show them what you would particularly like and from what part of the anatomy of the bird or animal concerned it comes from.

13

PREPARATION AND STORAGE OF MATERIALS

SKINNING

It is not an unduly difficult process for the fly-dresser to remove the skin of an animal and to treat it so that it will keep without becoming offensive. The skin is not being prepared as a taxidermist's specimen and the meticulous skill required for preparation for mounting or setting-up is not essential.

Needless to say the sooner after the death of the animal the skinning takes place the easier the task will be.

Lay the carcase of the animal on its back on a table or bench of convenient height and with a sharp knife make a shallow incision from the throat along the breast and belly to the vent. Then make four transverse cuts from the original incision down the insides of the legs.

It is very important to keep these cuts shallow and to avoid cutting into the flesh or guts.

Starting at one hind leg, with the thumbs open up the skin from the incisions a little at a time, if necessary using the point of the knife to ease it from any adhesions.

About halfway down the leg make a circular cut round the limb and the skin can be lifted clear. Repeat this on the other side.

The tail can now be either cut off at the root or slit down the underside and eased off the muscle and bone.

The skin should now be pulled forwards up to the front legs, which are treated in the same way as the rear. A final circular cut round the collar and the skin should be off in one piece.

Stretch the skin out hair side downwards on a piece of wood or hardboard, securing it with tacks or drawing-pins, and carefully remove (using the knife if necessary) any flesh or fat that may still be adhering to it.

Stand it in the sun or in a warm dry place until it is thoroughly dry and then paint the pelt with a strong solution of commercial formalin, which will preserve the hide and prevent its becoming objectionable. Let it dry again and then cut out the portions that you wish to keep; destroy any useless rubbish.

You must remember that formalin is potent and dangerous stuff and must not be allowed to come into contact with your own skin, so wear rubber gloves when handling it. Needless to say, keep it securely out of reach of children.

A safer and probably equally effective alternative method is to rub the skin with powdered alum. In this case it may be easier to apply the alum before the skin dries.

The skin of a bird can be removed whole in much the same way, leaving the feathers unplucked. Part the feathers as you make the cuts down the breast and legs. When you come to deal with the wings you will have to cut them through the "elbow" joint.

If somebody gives you the neck of an old cockerel carrying good hackles, skin it as a "cape" rather than pluck it. Slit down the underside of the gullet, make circular cuts behind the ears and round the base of the cape and remove the skin in one piece. This should then be treated with preservative as in the case of a whole skin.

The tails of Grey Squirrels, which are extensively used by fly-dressers, will keep satisfactorily without further treatment if the skin is removed from the bone and thoroughly dried. Cut the tail off at the root. "Start" the skin by slitting it down for about three quarters of an inch on its underside and ease the skin away from the flesh at its base. With one hand grip the tail very firmly at this eased portion, wrap the exposed end of muscle and bone with a piece of dry cloth or paper and with the other hand give it a strong steady pull. If the tail is reasonably fresh the skin will slide off in one clean piece.

Alternatively, leave the tail on the carcase but make a shallow cut through the skin right round the base of the tail. Now get a piece of springy sapling such as hazel about nine inches long and split this to about three inches from one end. Open this up and slip it over the base of the tail just aft of the cut. Hold the two split ends of sapling together and draw it thus tightened towards the tip of the tail. Again, the tail should then come off cleanly.

There are a couple of final points to be borne in mind before leaving this subject of skinning.

First, you may possibly find especially if the body is fresh that it carries "passengers" in the form of fleas, lice or mites, so the skin should be treated with an appropriate insecticide before being brought into the house.

The other point is that skinning an animal, or for that matter gutting a fish, can be a dirty job which can leave an unpleasant smell on the hands. If after completing such a task the hands are washed in hot water it seems to open the pores and allow the stench to penetrate and persist. To avoid this, get them as clean as possible first using cold water without soap.

DYEING

If feathers or fur of a particular colour are required they can of course be bought from the suppliers, but it is not difficult for the amateur to do his own dyeing quite successfully if certain elementary points are borne in mind.

First, always use rainwater or soft water. In many districts the mains supply is very "hard" and also been chemically treated, which can have disconcerting effects on the resulting colour. You can test this by dyeing two samples of the same material in separate solutions of the same dye made with rainwater and mains water. The difference can be very marked, for example the bright blue of "Teal and Blue" may come out as a dingy turquoise in hard water.

While many books quote interesting old recipes using various vegetable and mineral matter, a more satisfactory result will almost certainly be obtained by using a good quality dye which has been manufactured for this purpose. A number of firms supply dyes in powder form in a very wide range of colours, and concentrated dyes in liquid form are also available; the "Dylon" range is very effective.

It is of course essential that the material to be dyed is clean and free from grease and this involves thorough washing beforehand. Care must however be taken that the detergent or de-greasing agent does not take the natural "life" out of the material. Very thorough rinsing must be carried out.

Follow closely the makers' instructions on the dye package and check that the colour is satisfactory by testing it with a small piece of the material to be dyed before adding the "fixing" element (vinegar for Veniards' powder dyes and common salt for "Dylon" liquid). It is as well to remember in this connection that the colour of the wet material will be considerably darker than when it has dried.

"Mixing" colours is not the simple affair that it is with a child's paint-box: these dyes are chemicals and different colours may react differently. Equal quantities of red and blue may not necessarily produce purple.

Do not attempt to dye differing sorts of material in the same batch of dye solution. Some materials, for example the water-resistant feathers of Geese or other waterfowl, do not take up the dye as readily as others and will emerge as a paler shade.

If you want a good black, choose feather or fur that is already brown or coloured, the darker the better. White or very pale material will not take on an intense black. Some items are particularly difficult in this regard, especially Grey Squirrel tails which need a long period in a very strong solution of dye to give a satisfactory result.

Rinse and re-rinse the dyed material until no trace of colour comes away. If this is not done carefully the colour may "run" and spoil other material with which it may come into contact.

It is best to carry out your dyeing operations in an enamel, rather than bare metal, vessel. An old enamel grill-pan, being fairly wide and shallow, is more satisfactory than a deeper and narrower saucepan, particularly for the longer feathers.

Lastly, if you are doing your dyeing in the family kitchen be careful not to spill any of the dye, particularly once the fixing agent has been added: it is surprising how effective this can prove in the wrong place!

BLEACHING

From time to time one reads recommendations to bleach feathers or hair in order to remove the original pigment before dyeing them, but I am extremely dubious of this practice. Bleaching agents are complicated to handle and if they are powerful enough to take out the natural pigment they must surely have a deleterious effect on the "life" and texture of the material.

STORAGE OF MATERIALS

Quite apart from incurring the displeasure of the lady of the house by leaving feathers etc about, not omitting the cardinal offence of getting fish-hooks in the vacuum-cleaner, it is in the interests of the fly-dresser himself that his materials should be neatly and properly stored and readily available when required.

The ideal for this is a cabinet with close-fitting drawers. Wing and tail feathers, after sorting and grading, should be kept flat in closed transparent envelopes. While it is preferable to keep cock hackles "on skin" and to put the capes flat into separate transparent envelopes, loose hackles are best kept in airtight tins which should of course be clearly labelled.

Fur should always be kept "on skin" if possible and the pieces of pelt stored flat in transparent envelopes.

The principal enemy of both feathers and fur is the clothes-moth and it is advisable to put one of the proprietary anti-moth tablets in each drawer or box used for storage. Even when this precaution has been taken it is advisable to inspect your materials at frequent intervals to check their condition.

Seal's fur, dyed in various colours, is usually supplied in the form of cut fibres. A comparatively small quantity of this will make a large number of flies and a convenient container to accommodate the various colours can easily be made.

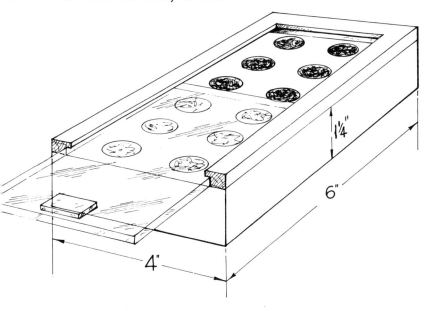

Get a smooth block of close-grained wood about 6 inches by 4 inches and about 1¼ inches deep and bore in it a dozen smooth holes about 1 inch deep and ¾ of an inch in diameter to take the colours commonly used. Press the fur down into these holes and when a particular colour is required just pinch out the amount needed.

The container will be a neater and more efficient job if you can fit it with a sliding lid, preferably of clear "Perspex".

Care should be taken with the storage of your other materials.

Silk, both tying-silk and floss, deteriorates rapidly in strong light and should be kept in closed containers. Do not forget to anchor the loose end in the notch cut in the flange of the reel if subsequent tangling is to be avoided.

Tinsels will also tarnish rapidly if left exposed to the air and should likewise be kept in closed containers.

Varnish. In addition to the risk of leaking and spoiling other materials, varnish will rapidly evaporate and harden if bottle caps are not screwed down properly. Try to keep the bottle upright when not in use. (See page 33).

Hooks should of course be protected against rust (unlikely to be a serious problem in a reasonably dry house) and care should be taken to keep the various sizes separate in clearly labelled containers. Left loose they can become a real hazard to small children and domestic pets.

PART V

BOOKS AND ORGANISATIONS

14

THE FLY-DRESSER'S BOOKSHELF

As a visit to any Public Library will soon convince you, fly-dressing is a well documented subject and books on it are as numerous as they are variable in quality.

The criticism that can be levelled at many of these is that their authors have tended to assume that their potential readers are already very knowledgeable on the subject and that such books do not make their points sufficiently clear to the uninitiated.

However, our fly-dresser should make room on his shelves for some of the standard works, reference to one or the other of which should produce the answer to most of his queries.

To my mind the following are well worth such a place:
BOOKS ON THE ACTUAL PROCESSES OF DRESSING
Fly-tying for Beginners, by Geoffrey Bucknall, published by E. M. Art Publishing Co., Peterborough.

This is an excellent clear guide for the beginner.

Fly-tying Problems and their Answers by John Veniard, published by A. & C. Black.

Everyone strikes snags at some time in their fly-tying career and this will dispose of most of them.

All-fur Flies and how to dress them, by W. H. Lawrie, published by Pelham Books.
A clear and useful guide to the use of fur and hair.

How to dress Salmon Flies, by T. E. Pryce-Tannatt, published by A. & C. Black.
For the man interested in tying the old traditional fully-dressed salmon-flies this book will give most of the answers.

BOOKS LISTING SPECIFIC DRESSINGS
A Fly-dresser's Guide, by John Veniard, published by A. & C. Black.

This can be backed up by the same author's:
A Further Guide to Fly-dressing and *Reservoir and Lake Flies*, both again published by A. & C. Black.

Another standard work on this subject is:
A Dictionary of Trout Flies, by A. Courtney Williams, also published by A. & C. Black.

BOOKS ON ENTOMOLOGY
As mentioned on various occasions in this book, many of our flies are deliberate attempts to imitate a natural insect and our efforts are bound to have triggered off a subsidiary interest in the insects themselves.

Many excellent books have been written on this subject, including Courtney Williams' famous "Dictionary" referred to in the preceding note. I would also recommend:
The Angler's Entomology, by J. R. Harris, published by Collins.

Lake Flies and their Imitation, by Lt.-Cdr. C. F. Walker, published by Herbert Jenkins.

Trout Flies of Still Water and *Trout Fly Recognition*, both by John Goddard and published by A. & C. Black.

These last two are worth the money for the illustrations alone; some of the underwater photographs are remarkable.

While it is recognised that some of these volumes may now be out of print, it may be possible to obtain copies in good condition from one of the firms of booksellers who specialise in this class of book. Several of these firms advertise regularly in the angling press.

Two of several to be recommended are:

> R. J. W. Coleby,
>   Barrashead House,
>   Lochmaben,
>   Dumfriesshire,
>   Scotland.

> Grayling Books,
>   Lyvennet,
>   Crosby Ravensworth,
>   Penrith,
>   Cumbria.

15

SOME USEFUL ORGANISATIONS

The Association of Professional Game Angling Instructors.
    Secretary: J. A. Martin, Esq. J.P.
        26 Ling Hill,
        Newby,
        Scarborough.

This association was formed by Lt.-Col. Esmond Drury and others in 1968 with the object of raising the standards of instruction. It admits to its membership those qualified to teach casting and fly-tying (either or both).

The Fly-dressers' Guild.
    Membership Secretary:
        H. A. Reid, Esq.
        18 St. Michael's Crescent,
        Pinner,
        Middlesex.

Founded in 1969 by a group of enthusiasts in the Winchester area, the Guild now has a wide, even international, membership.

In addition to organising demonstrations and competitions, it issues a monthly newsletter providing a very lively forum for the exchange of ideas and experiences.

Many magazines often include articles on various aspects of fly-dressing which are often interesting and instructive. It can be worth while to cut these out and file them in an alphabetical index.

The primary reason for tying flies is to catch fish, and fish can only thrive in a clean environment. To help in the continual fight against pollution every self-respecting angler ought to support:

> The Anglers' Co-operative Association,
> Midland Bank Chambers,
> Westgate,
> Grantham.

An organisation which carries out a great deal of research and other activities for the development of salmon and trout fisheries is:

> The Salmon and Trout Association,
> Fishmongers' Hall,
> London, E.C.4.

With a somewhat wider scope, that of field sports in general, the following is also worthy of support:

> The British Field Sports Society,
> 59 Kennington Road,
> London, SE1.

INDEX

169